ULTIMATE Explorer GUIDE

EXPLORE, DISCOVER, and CREATE your own adventures with real National Geographic Explorers

Nancy Honovich

Foreword by Lee Berger

NATIONAL GEOGRAPHIC

WASHINGTON, D.C.

CONTENTS

SKY

FOREWORD

The world is full of mystery. As a paleoanthropologist, I try to uncover the answers to some of those mysteries by searching for traces of early human ancestors and relatives. Every discovery we make in this field is noteworthy, because it brings us closer to understanding the origins of humanity—and just what it is that makes us human! Over the past few years, however, two of my teams' discoveries have also been notable for different reasons.

The first of these occurred in a limestone cave called Malapa, situated in the dry grasslands outside of Johannesburg, South Africa. We had unearthed the remains of a previously undiscovered early human relative now known as *Australopithecus sediba*. But what made this find even more remarkable was that it wasn't me who found the first fossil—it was my son, Matthew! Only nine years old at the time, he had uncovered a completely new species of human ancestor.

The second major discovery uncovered yet another previously unknown relative in our family tree: *Homo naledi*. However, this discovery was extra surprising because of its location. *Homo naledi* was found in the Rising Star cave in Johannesburg, South Africa—one of the most popular and explored caving systems in Africa. Thousands of people had been exploring these caves for fun over the past 50 years but had never noticed what was right before them!

Put together, these two finds point to something incredible: There are endless important discoveries waiting to be uncovered right under our noses, and anyone can find them—even you. But to find more of these amazing discoveries, the world needs explorers. And not just in the field of paleoanthropology; from marine life to new technologies to far-off planets, we have so much more to learn about the universe around us. And some of the best people to find these discoveries are kids just like you. So what are you waiting for? Dig into the *Ultimate Explorer Guide* and get exploring!

— Professor Lee Berger
National Geographic Explorer-in-Residence

HOW TO USE THIS BOOK

Throughout this book you'll meet many real-life explorers who will give you a behind-the-scenes look at their work and share tips on what you can do to become an explorer.

On Location takes you along on major science explorations that have occurred around the world.

Text and colorful photos provide key details about each object, animal, or concept that was or is currently being explored.

Explore Now! offers simple actions you can take to better understand and explore a featured subject.

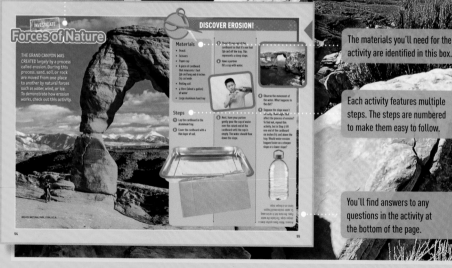

To make sense of a subject he or she is studying, an explorer must understand the science behind it. **Investigate** features a detailed hands-on activity you can perform to understand a key science concept that you are exploring in a chapter.

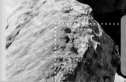

The materials you'll need for the activity are identified in this box.

Each activity features multiple steps. The steps are numbered to make them easy to follow.

You'll find answers to any questions in the activity at the bottom of the page.

Be a ... features an activity or simple tips you can follow to begin your work as an explorer of a particular subject.

The **title** tells you about an area of exploration that will be discussed in a chapter.

There are many different jobs in each area of exploration. In the **Help Wanted** section, you'll learn about four. Each includes a description of the job, details about the work-place, and requirements you'll need to get hired.

Challenge sections allow you to put yourself in the shoes of a professional explorer. You'll examine various clues—in the form of images and text—to solve a mystery.

Answer keys can be found at the bottom of the page.

Did You Know? text blocks throughout the book offer fun and surprising facts about the topic of the spread.

LAND

ATTENTION, LAND LOVERS!

Grab your hiking shoes and get ready to trek around the globe. You'll explore extreme landforms, wild beasts, unique cultures, and so much more.

ANATOLIA, TURKEY

EXPLORE
the Wild

THERE ARE MILLIONS OF different animal species in the world. With so many diverse critters, who can keep track of them all? Animal explorers! These dedicated scientists and researchers travel the globe to track and study animals' every move. They investigate the food animals eat, the places they live, and the ways they interact with other creatures—including humans. Learning this information helps the experts identify issues that threaten the existence of wildlife. And by knowing these issues, they can better defend the lives of all animals on Earth.

So what does it take to be a wildlife explorer? Read on to find out.

HELP WANTED

If you can't get enough of furry felines or bug out when you see a stick insect, you might consider a career in wildlife exploration. Check out some of these animal-related jobs:

ZOOLOGIST

Responsibilities: Zoologists are scientists who study the behaviors and physical characteristics of animals. They observe how animals interact with one another and their environment, and they share their findings with conservation groups and the public. Some zoologists focus on certain groups of animals such as mammals, lizards, or amphibians.

Workplace: Zoos, research labs, universities and colleges, and wildlife reserves

What you need: Patience, a love of animals, and a degree in zoology, biology, or other animal-related science

WILDLIFE PHOTOGRAPHER

Responsibilities: These photographers specialize in snapping photos of animals in their natural surroundings.

Workplace: News agencies or publishing companies. Some photographers work for themselves and have their photos featured and sold in museums and galleries.

What you need: Patience, a love of animals and the outdoors, a camera, and photography skills

Wichita Eagle

BE AN ... ANIMAL EXPERT!

Although you may not be able to jet off to the jungles of South America or the Arctic tundra to study wildlife just yet, you can still study wildlife in your own neighborhood using some of the same tricks professional explorers use. Here's how.

Materials

- Binoculars
- Camera
- A journal and pen to jot down your observations
- Clothing to blend in with your surroundings
- Watch or stopwatch
- White bedsheet for a screen
- Sunblock
- Sun hat

Steps

1. Find the perfect spot. Animals are usually drawn to trees, shrubs, and bright flowers, so look for a place in your neighborhood where you might find such plants.

2. Now that you've found a spot, cover up! Many animals are afraid of humans and will run away if they detect you. So cover yourself in a sheet or blanket, or wear clothing that helps you blend in with the environment. Try to keep as still and quiet as possible.

3. When you see an animal, observe it carefully. What is it doing? Is it eating something? Is it interacting with other animals? At what time of day is this happening? How long does the action go on? Take notes of everything you observe.

4. Can you identify the animal? If not, take a photo or draw a picture of it. You can use the picture as a reference to look it up online or in a book.

5. Each day, return to the same spot. Repeat Step 2 through 4. Then look at your notes. Do you see any patterns?

CAUTION!

Wild animals are unpredictable and can attack when they feel threatened. Never approach an animal in the wild.

WILDLIFE CONSERVATIONIST

Responsibilities: Wildlife conservationists are experts who come up with ways to protect animals and plants, and the places they live. This may involve relocating animals to safer places, working with governments to establish protected areas, and alerting the public to major problems.

Workplace: Government and nonprofit wildlife conservation groups

What you need: A passion for animals, good communication skills, and a degree in zoology, forestry, ecology, or a similar field

VETERINARIAN

Responsibilities: Veterinarians are medical experts who specialize in the health of animals. They treat diseases and injuries.

Workplace: Mainly animal hospitals and clinics

What you need: A degree in veterinary science, patience, a love of animals, the ability to tolerate noisy environments, and the ability to work well with frightened or sick animals

13

Animals Around the World

IF YOU WANT TO BE A WILDLIFE EXPLORER, you'll have to become a pro at studying how animals thrive in their natural environments. This includes learning about the body parts and behaviors that help an organism survive in its habitat. For example, bison have thick coats to keep warm during cold winters on the plains, while camels have fat-storing humps that allow them to go for long stretches in the desert without eating.

Check out some of the world's major habitats, and discover what it takes for an animal to survive there.

Tropical Rain Forests

WHAT THEY ARE: Tropical rain forests, found near Earth's Equator, are warm areas that get more than eight feet (2.5 m) of rain each year. These conditions produce tall trees with dense foliage, so you have to look very closely to spot wildlife.

WHAT LIVES THERE: Many animals have adapted to life in the trees. Capuchin and spider monkeys have long limbs to help them swing from branches. Toucans have large beaks, which they use to grab fruit on high branches.

Deserts

WHAT THEY ARE: Deserts are regions that receive less than 10 inches (25 cm) of rain each year. Many deserts, like the Sahara in Africa, experience scorching temperatures during the day. However, some deserts, like Mongolia's Gobi, can be chilly year-round.

WHAT LIVES THERE: Many animals that live in hot deserts—such as kangaroo rats and badgers—avoid the daytime heat and are active only at night. Other creatures, such as horned lizards, have thick skin to lock in any water they consume.

Grasslands

WHAT THEY ARE: Grasslands are flat, open areas with wild grasses and few trees. Some grasslands, like those in India and Kenya, are tropical. That means that they are warm year-round and have a wet and dry season. Others, like the plains of North America, are temperate. This means they have hot summers and cold winters.

WHAT LIVES THERE: Many grassland dwellers, such as prairie dogs and badgers, have brown or gray coats that help them blend in with the vegetation, so you have to look closely to spot them. During the dry season, you'll find many animals around watering holes.

Temperate and Coniferous Forests

WHAT THEY ARE: Temperate forests are those that experience all four seasons and have tall trees with broad leaves. Coniferous forests undergo short, moist summers and long, cold winters.

WHAT LIVES THERE: In temperate forests, animals need to adapt to the changing seasons. During warmer months, squirrels and chipmunks bury nuts for winter snacking. In coniferous forests, black bears can be seen chowing down on berries, roots, and grasses during summer. In winter, they escape the cold by hibernating.

Tundra

WHAT IT IS: The tundra is a cold and snowy region that spans the Arctic Circle. Temperatures here can dip below freezing for 10 months a year. Winter temperatures often reach minus 40°F (-40°C). Brrr!

WHAT LIVES THERE: You have to look extra closely to see signs of life. That's because many animals, such as polar bears and arctic foxes, appear white to blend in with the snow. This helps them avoid being detected by predators and prey. The animals also use their thick winter coats to help keep warm.

EXPLORE NOW!

In addition to their thick woolly coats, bison also have another adaptation that keeps them warm: They generate body heat while huddling in groups. To investigate how this works, try this:

> Grab six water bottles, two thermometers, a large rubber band, and modeling clay.

> Fill all the water bottles with warm water. Bind five of them together with a large rubber band. Remove the cap from the center bottle and insert a thermometer. To keep the thermometer in place, put a piece of modeling clay in the mouth of the bottle.

> Remove the cap of the sixth bottle. Put the second thermometer inside, with a piece of clay to hold it in place. Keep this bottle away from the others.

> Record the temperatures on both thermometers. Then leave the bottles alone for 20 minutes. Return to check the temperatures. Which bottle is warmer: the one in the pack or the one standing alone?

15

Animal Migrations

IF YOU LIVE NEAR JACKSON HOLE, WYOMING, U.S.A., chances are you've noticed bands of pronghorn antelope disappear in the winter and then return in the spring. Where do they go? The pronghorn are migrating, or moving from one place to another, to find food. Many animals make similar treks. Some migrate to find food and water. Others do so to find mates or escape the cold winter.

Check out some of the animal kingdom's most well-known land migrations.

Mountain Goats *Oreamnos americanus*

Mountain goats in the northwestern United States and Canada can be found on high mountain slopes in the spring and summer. During the winter, strong winds and snowdrifts can make these areas challenging, so the goats move down the mountain.

Porcupine Caribou *Rangifer tarandus granti*

In early spring, Porcupine caribou make their way to the coastal plain of Alaska, U.S.A., and the Yukon of Canada. There they give birth to caribou calves. By late summer, the area becomes infested with pesky mosquitoes, so the caribou leave the region and travel up to 300 miles (483 km) into the foothills and mountains of Alaska and Canada.

EXPLORE NOW!

How do explorers know when and where to spot migrating animals? They do their research! Go online to find out what animals will be migrating through your town and when. Then mark your calendars.

Wildebeest *Connochaetes taurinus*

Wildebeest are large mammals that can often be found in the Serengeti, a region in eastern Africa. During the region's wet season there is plenty of grass for the animals to feed on. But in May or June, the dry season begins. So, the wildebeest stampede north in search of greener pastures and water. More than one million wildebeest take part in this epic migration, which spans 1,800 miles (2,897 km).

Red Crab *Gecarcoidea natalis*

For most of the year, red crabs live on the rain forest floor of Australia's Christmas Island. Around December, when the wet season begins, millions of crabs leave the rain forest and head to the coast. To get to their destination, the crabs cross roads, often causing traffic to stop! When they reach the coast, the crabs breed and release their eggs into the sea.

Emperor Penguins *Aptenodytes forsteri*

Emperor penguins spend most of their time diving for food off the coast of Antarctica. But each March, they leave the ocean and travel 50 miles (80.5 km) inland to their breeding grounds. There, the female lays an egg. While the male keeps the egg warm, the female travels back to the ocean to feed on fish, squid, and krill. She returns two months later, when the baby chick hatches. Then she regurgitates, or throws up, her fishy meal into the hatchling's mouth.

On the Right Track

IF YOU'RE STRUGGLING TO SPOT WILDLIFE, the time of day might have something to do with it. Animals aren't always active when the sun is shining. Sometimes, they creep out at night when they're less likely to be seen. So, how do you know if you've had any nighttime visitors in your neighborhood? Look for animal tracks. Soil, snow, sand, and dew-covered surfaces all provide a great canvas for animals to scamper across. Can you identify the animal tracks shown here?

 A

The paw prints of this large animal can measure up to nine inches (23 cm) across. Because this animal is usually snoozing during cold-weather months, these tracks were likely made in the spring or summer.

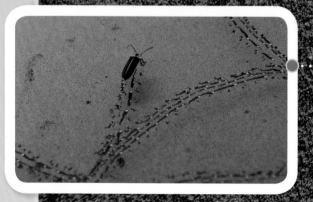

B

These tiny tracks were left on a car windshield covered with dew. The critter that's responsible for them has its own light source.

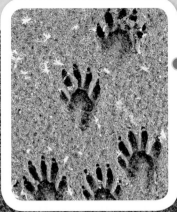

C
This animal is known for its bandit-like appearance. It was likely prowling for fruit, seeds, or bird eggs when it made these paw prints.

The hooves of this animal are made of keratin—the same material that makes up human nails and hair. They also leave deep impressions in the mud.

D

This animal doesn't have any feet, but that doesn't stop it from getting around. It lies on its belly and uses a sidewinding motion to travel.

E

F

If these two sets of tracks look different, it's because they are. The tracks on the right were made by a small furry creature known for its pointy ears and cottonlike tail. The tracks on the left were made by a larger animal with a long nose and sharp teeth.

BONUS: Can you guess what was happening in this photo?

Answers: A: brown bear, B: firefly, C: raccoon, D: deer, E: snake, F: (right) rabbit, (left) timber wolf. BONUS: The timber wolf was most likely hunting the rabbit.

MEET AN EXPLORER

WHO: Emma Stokes

JOB: Wildlife researcher and conservationist

What inspired you to choose this profession?

I was always interested in wildlife from an early age and loved watching nature documentaries on TV. But my real interest started a bit later, when I decided to join a wildlife research expedition to Africa. Being able to get directly involved and experience these issues firsthand got me really hooked.

Why was the discovery of 125,000 western lowland gorillas in central Africa in 2007 so important?

This discovery increased the total number of gorillas that we knew were living in the forests of central Africa. This is important, as gorillas are vulnerable to many threats—such as poaching for food and also diseases like Ebola—and their numbers had been declining quite rapidly in recent years. Discovering a larger population than we previously thought is good news for conservation!

How did you count these gorillas?

Western lowland gorillas are actually really hard to see because they live in dense forests. They are not used to people and will typically run away from humans. So, as a result, we don't actually count the individual gorillas—what we count are the signs they leave behind. Gorillas make a nest every night to sleep in—sometimes in the trees and sometimes on the ground. As gorillas are quite large, the nests are visible to teams of researchers walking in the forest. With training, we are able to reliably count them. We then apply a mathematical formula to convert the number of nests into the number of individual gorillas that made them.

What's the difference between tiger conservation and gorillas?

Unlike gorillas, tigers are top predators, so in addition to protecting them, you also need to think about protecting the animals they need to eat for food and to ensure the tigers have enough space to live. There are only about 3,200 wild tigers left in Asia, and they only live in a few places. By identifying and focusing on those places where tigers have the best chance of survival—where they have enough space and where they can have enough to eat—we are helping ensure the best chance possible of increasing the number of tigers in the wild.

Have you had any unusual experiences while in the field?

Yes, many! Sometimes you get to see amazing behaviors—like the first time we saw twins being born to western gorillas—and sometimes you get to see really unusual encounters or rare sightings, like the time I saw a crocodile attacking a gorilla in a swamp (the gorilla escaped, but it gave him a bit of a fright).

How could a reader help endangered animals?

You can actually do a lot right in your own hometown. You can create awareness of important wildlife issues in your local communities and schools, or lobby your local government representative or congressperson on important wildlife issues. You can get involved in campaigns that encourage people not to buy products that are harmful to wildlife or that contain ingredients that threaten important wildlife habitats. For example, many products we buy in the supermarkets contain palm oil, which comes from plantations in Asia that have cleared forest habitats that are important for wildlife such as orangutans.

What advice would you give to kids who want to make this a career?

Get directly involved in whatever way you can, either through a local wildlife club or by getting involved in a local wildlife campaign in your town. Hands-on experience is really valuable, as it will help you better understand the issues and help you decide what aspects of wildlife conservation you are interested in and what you enjoy.

To the Rescue

ACCORDING TO THE INTERNATIONAL UNION for the Conservation of Nature, almost 20,000 species are threatened with extinction. Learn what conservationists are doing to bring these five back from the brink.

Lemur Leaf Frog *Agalychnis lemur*

STATUS: Critically endangered

BACKGROUND: The lemur leaf frog, which is native to Colombia, Costa Rica, and Panama, has experienced a rapid decline in population. A deadly disease caused by a type of fungus—an organism that breaks down other organisms for nutrients—is to blame.

ACTION: In 2001, the Atlanta Botanical Garden began a breeding program to boost the frog's population. Since then, other zoos have also joined the effort.

Giant Panda *Ailuropoda melanoleuca*

STATUS: Endangered

BACKGROUND: The bamboo forests of China are home to giant pandas. Over the years, loggers have cleared these forests to make way for farmland and transportation. As a result, the pandas' natural habitat has diminished—and so has their population. A recent study showed that there are fewer than 1,900 giant pandas in the wild.

ACTION: The Chinese government has established protected areas called reserves, where no one is allowed to harm the animals or their environment. Breeding centers have also been created to help the pandas mate and reproduce.

EXPLORE NOW!

You don't have to be a professional explorer to help endangered animals. Here's what you can do now:

> You can reduce greenhouse gas emissions by powering off electronics that you're not using and encouraging adults to ride bikes instead of drive.

> Spread the word: Educate people about animals that are endangered. The more they know, the more they can do something to help.

> Write a letter to the mayor of your town (or another elected official) encouraging him or her to take action. You can find your mayor's address on your city's website.

Black Rhino *Diceros bicornis*

STATUS: Critically endangered

BACKGROUND: Until the mid-1900s, more than 70,000 black rhinos roamed freely across parts of South Africa. However, things changed when poachers began to illegally hunt and kill these animals for their horns. By the late 1990s, only 2,400 black rhinos remained in the wild.

ACTION: In 2003, conservationists at the World Wildlife Fund (WWF) began moving the animals to a safer environment protected by security. Because the rhinos' new home is 900 miles (1,448 km) away, the conservationists have resorted to airlifting the animals by helicopter!

Red Wolf *Canis rufus*

STATUS: Critically endangered

BACKGROUND: Red wolves could once be found throughout the southeastern United States, but over time they were hunted nearly to extinction. By the 1980s, only 17 red wolves remained in the wild!

ACTION: Scientists captured the last 17 wolves and took them to a wildlife refuge, where they bred the wolves in captivity. Slowly, they are beginning to see the results of their efforts. There are now more than 100 red wolves in the wild.

Polar Bear *Ursus maritimus*

STATUS: Vulnerable

BACKGROUND: Polar bears live in the Arctic, where they rely on sea ice for many things. The bears use it as platforms to stand on while they monitor the frigid waters for signs of food. They also mate and give birth on the ice. In recent years, rising temperatures have caused the ice to melt, leaving little ground for the polar bears.

ACTION: According to scientists, a buildup of greenhouse gases in the atmosphere is causing temperatures to rise. These gases are caused by human actions such as driving cars, using electricity, and throwing away garbage. Conservationists are supporting research on climate change and encouraging governments to find ways to curb greenhouse gas emissions.

The World of Worms

YOU DON'T ALWAYS HAVE TO GO OUTDOORS to see wildlife in action. Sometimes, you can observe nature in your own home. Put your observation skills to the test by building an awesome earthy castle fit for the ultimate dirt kings: worms.

BUILD A WORM CASTLE!

Materials

- A large, clean, empty jar
- Pebbles
- A cup of soil and peat moss mixture (available at most nurseries)
- Spray bottle of water
- Food scraps such as apple cores, banana peels, eggshells, coffee grinds, and bread crumbs
- Two to three worms from your garden or a bait store
- An adult with a drill
- A sheet of dark construction paper
- Tape
- Writing materials

Steps

1. Ask an adult to drill four small holes in the lid of the jar. Place the lid aside.

2. Add pebbles to your jar until the bottom is completely covered.

3. Pour the soil and peat moss mixture into the jar.

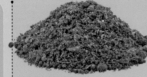

4. Spritz the soil mixture until it is damp. Be careful not to soak it.

5. Invite the worms to the castle by placing them gently into the jar.

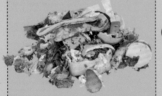

6. Next, add the food scraps to the bottle. This is your worm food.

7. Place the lid on the jar.

8. Worms are sensitive to light, so grab the dark construction paper and wrap it around the jar. Secure the paper with a piece of tape.

9. Place the jar in a cool, dark place.

10. Using your writing materials, describe the worm castle you created. Be sure to include information about the worms, the food you provided, and the soil.

11. After three days, remove the construction paper. Look into your worm castle. Record your observations. Be sure to note the following:

    → What does the soil look like?

    → What have the worms been doing?

    → What happened to the food?

12. Repeat Steps 8 and 9.

13. Repeat Step 11 every three days for the next two weeks. If the food supply starts to dwindle, add more food scraps to the jar.

14. After two weeks, release your worms into a yard.

Here are a few things you might see: As earthworms move, they make tunnels through the soil. The food starts to diminish as the worms eat it. Worm poop, called castings, looks like bunches of little grapes and will likely appear on the soil surface. Castings help fertilize the soil.

EXPLORE
Ancient Animals

NOT ALL WILDLIFE EXPLORERS STUDY ANIMALS that are living today. Some prefer animals of the past. They travel the world searching for fossils, or preserved remains, of ancient life-forms such as dinosaurs, woolly mammoths, saber-toothed cats, and more. By studying these remains, they can learn what life was like eons ago. This information is important because it helps us understand why some life-forms died out and others survived—and evolved—over time. Experts can then use this information to anticipate and prepare for changes that can have a huge effect on present-day life.

A DINOSAUR MODEL IN VIENNA, AUSTRIA

HELP WANTED

Make no bones about it: If you're into dinosaurs and other types of ancient life, there are plenty of careers for you to choose from. Here are a few:

PALEONTOLOGIST

Responsibilities: Paleontologists are scientists who study the different forms of life that existed over time. Many paleontologists go on digs to uncover fossils and then study them in lab.

Workplace: Outdoors, museums, universities, labs

What you need: A love of travel, camping, and the great outdoors. You'll also need a degree in paleontology or a similar field. Good writing skills will help you explain your findings.

PALEOBOTANIST

Responsibilities: Paleobotanists are scientists who study the remains of ancient plants. The information they uncover helps us understand how modern plants evolved.

Workplace: Outdoors, museums, universities, labs, and private companies

What you need: A love of travel, camping, and the great outdoors is helpful. A degree in biology, geology, or similar field is essential.

BE A ... PALEONTOLOGIST!

Materials

- Rock identification book
- Fossil identification book
- Note-taking materials
- Geology hammer
- Pick
- Steel chisel
- Hard hat
- Goggles
- Gloves

Steps

1. Do some research. Read about different types of fossils and how they form. Get to know these fossils so that you know what you're looking for. Also, do some research on sedimentary rocks, where many fossils are found.

2. Have an adult help you find a dig. Contact the nearest natural history museum for information about fossil digs in your area. You can also check out the National Park Service website at nps.gov to learn more.

3. Grab your gear and your adult and head to your fossil dig. At your destination, search for sedimentary rocks. Although most of these rocks will be buried, some will be exposed along riverbanks, cliffs, quarries, and desert badlands.

4. Carefully inspect the layers of rock for bonelike structures or imprints of body parts or plant materials. Use a magnifying glass for a closer look.

NOTE: If you find a fossil in a park or protected area, leave it alone. Make a note of its location. Then report it to park officials.

5. If you are allowed to dig up the fossil, put on your goggles and gloves. Then grab your tools and carefully chip away at the rock surrounding the fossil.

6. Gently remove the fossil from the rock, wrap it in toilet paper, and place it in a resealable plastic sandwich bag for safekeeping.

7. Take notes about your find. Record the date and type of fossil you found. Make comments about the location and weather. Then sketch the fossil.

CAUTION!

Quarries and riverbanks can be dangerous, so never go fossil hunting without an adult.

SCIENCE JOURNALIST

Responsibilities: Science journalists are writers who report important findings. For example, they may write about a major dinosaur discovery or expedition. Their articles may appear in newspapers, magazines, and websites.

Workplace: Anywhere

What you need: The ability to write is a must. A college degree in journalism with an emphasis in a particular science is usually required. Good interviewing skills are also helpful.

DIORAMA ARTIST

Responsibilities: Diorama artists are those who work with scientists to create models for museum exhibitions. These models can include reproductions of ancient animals in their natural settings. They may also paint backdrops or murals.

Workplace: Museums

What you need: A fine arts degree is essential. Past experience working or volunteering in a museum is helpful.

Figuring Out Fossils

SO WHY ARE FOSSILS SUCH A BIG DEAL? Sure, they tell us a lot about the past. But what makes them so exciting is how rare they are. When most animals die, they get eaten by other organisms. Over time, the leftover bones turn to dust.

But sometimes, the remains are preserved. This can happen for various reasons. To learn why, check out the following different fossils.

Petrified Fossils

BACKGROUND: When most people think of fossils, they think *T. rex* teeth and *Allosaurus* claws. Most of these fossils are "petrified," which means they have been turned to stone. For a petrified fossil to form, the animal must be buried in sediment, such as volcanic ash or silt, shortly after it dies. Then mineral-rich water must pass through the sediment until it reaches the dead animal's body. Over time, two things can happen: The water may dissolve the animal's remains and replace them with minerals, or the water will seep into tiny pores in the animal's bones, where it deposits minerals. The end result is a stony fossil.

WHERE TO FIND THEM: Petrified Forest National Park in Arizona, U.S.A.; Yellowstone National Park; the Canadian Rockies; the badlands of North Dakota, U.S.A.

Molds and Casts

BACKGROUND: Mold fossils form when an organism completely dissolves in sedimentary rock and leaves behind an imprint in the rock. This imprint, or mold, is in the shape of the organism. A cast forms after water has deposited minerals and sediment inside the mold. These deposited materials fill the empty space and make a cast. Explorers have discovered many mold and cast fossils of ammonites, an extinct mollusk.

WHERE TO FIND THEM: Coastal areas of the United Kingdom and riverbanks of the Potomac River in the eastern United States

Carbon Films

BACKGROUND: All living things contain an element called carbon. When an organism dies and is buried in many layers of sediment, heat and pressure can cause the organism to break down. If the organism doesn't have a hard skeleton, the only thing that will remain is a thin film of carbon. This carbon film shows delicate parts of the organism.

WHERE TO FIND THEM: Wheeler Shale near Delta, Utah, U.S.A., and parts of Germany

Preserved Remains

BACKGROUND: Some animals were preserved in their original state. This can happen in many ways. In some cases, a small organism, such as an insect, became trapped inside amber—a sticky tree resin. The resin hardened into amber and sealed the insect inside. Other animals fell into tar pits or became frozen in ice. These materials kept their bodies from decaying and kept them well-preserved.

WHERE TO FIND THEM: La Brea Tar Pits in California, U.S.A.; the Arctic tundra; the Baltic area of Europe; and northern parts of Siberia

Trace Fossils

BACKGROUND: Trace fossils are those that show the activities or behavior of an animal. They can include footprints, droppings, burrows, and more. Footprint fossils typically form when an animal steps in mud or sand. The footprints become buried in layers of sediment, which over time, harden into solid rock.

WHERE TO FIND THEM: United States: southwestern Arkansas, the border between Arizona and Utah, and other western states

EXPLORE NOW!

To learn how cast fossils are formed, try making one of your own. You'll need two paper cups, water, molding clay, plaster of Paris, and a small object that represents an animal, such as a toy dinosaur, twig, paper clip, or shell.

> Pour 1/4 cup (59 mL) water and 1/2 cup (100 g) plaster of Paris into the first cup. Mix the ingredients and place the cup aside for two minutes.

> Grab the second cup. Press some molding clay into the bottom of the cup. Use enough clay to fill an inch (2.5 cm) of the cup—this represents the earth or soil where your animal object died.

> Next, grab your animal object. Press the "animal" into the clay. Then remove it. This represents how an animal in sediment might completely dissolve.

> Pour your plaster of Paris mixture over the clay—this demonstrates how the minerals seep into the open spaces left by the organism. Let the mixture dry for 24 hours.

> After the mixture has dried, cut away the paper cup. Separate the plaster from the clay. Now you have a mold fossil!

Deep Inside Earth's Crust

SCIENTISTS USE SEVERAL METHODS to determine the age of a fossil. One involves identifying the part of Earth's crust in which the fossil was found.

Earth's continental crust, which stretches 25 miles (40 km) beneath the planet's surface, contains many different layers. Generally, the oldest fossils are found in the deepest layers of the crust, while the more recent remains are found closer to the surface.

Scientists have grouped the layers into three basic groups—Paleozoic, Mesozoic, and Cenozoic—which represent the past 542 million years of life.

EXPLORE NOW!

Most dinosaur names are made of different word parts. The word parts often refer to a characteristic of the dinosaur. Determine the meanings of the following dinosaur names.

DINOSAUR NAMES

> Triceratops
> Plateosaurus
> Brachyceratops
> Carnotaurus
> Oviraptor

WORD PART	MEANING
Brachy	Short
Carno	Meat-eater
Cera	Horn
Ovi	Egg
Plateo	Flat
Raptor	Thief
Saurus	Reptile
Taurus	Bull
Tops	Face
Tri	Three

TRICERATOPS

Answers: *Triceratops*: three-horned face; *Plateosaurus*: flat reptile; *Brachyceratops*: short-horned face; *Carnotaurus*: meat-eating bull; *Oviraptor*: egg thief

PALEOZOIC ERA

The Paleozoic era, which began 542 million years ago, represents one of the oldest geological periods. During this era, the oceans were populated with a variety of creatures. Vertebrates—animals with backbones—first appeared on land, as did the first trees and cockroaches!

TRILOBITE FOSSIL WITH SEA STARS

> **Trilobites** were armored sea creatures that lacked a backbone scuttled across the ocean floor.

> **Tetrapods** were vertebrates that looked like snakes or lizards roamed across the land. These creatures ranged in size from four inches (10 cm) to 16 feet (5 m).

> *Archimylacris eggintoni*, the cockroach's ancient ancestor, first appeared.

> *Archaeopteris*, the first trees, appeared, bearing fernlike leaves.

MESOZOIC ERA

The Mesozoic era, which began about 251 million years ago, is sometimes called the "age of reptiles." Dinosaurs appeared during the early part of this era and flourished. They died out at the end of the Mesozoic era, nearly 65 million years ago. The first birds and mammals also appeared in this era.

> *Nyasasaurus parringtoni* was one of the earliest dinosaurs. It stood on its hind legs and was about the size of a Labrador retriever. Woof!

> *Tyrannosaurus rex,* or "tyrant lizard king," terrorized the land with its powerful legs and sharp, banana-size teeth.

> *Maotherium asiaticus* was one of many mammals that appeared toward the end of the Mesozoic era. It was about the size of a chipmunk and likely fed on insects and worms.

> *Aurornis xui* is one of the earliest known birds. The feathered creature was flightless, and had a long tail and toothy jaws.

TYRANNOSAURUS REX

CENOZOIC ERA

The Cenozoic era, which began about 65 million years ago, is the most recent geologic era. The era is sometimes called the "age of mammals" because mammals flourished during this time.

> **Saber-toothed cats** were feline creatures known for their long, sharp canine teeth. Some of these animals were the size of bobcats.

> **Woolly mammoths** were elephant-like mammals that sported woolly coats and extra-long tusks that grew up to 15 feet (4.6 m) in length.

> The earliest humans also appeared during this era. Scientists recently dug up a jawbone in Ethiopia. They estimate the fossil is 2.8 million years old.

WOOLLY MAMMOTH

MEET AN EXPLORER

WHO: Nizar Ibrahim

JOB: Paleontologist

When Nizar Ibrahim was five years old, he received a book about dinosaurs. He was so fascinated by it that he was determined to write his own book about the subject one day. He even wrote his name under the author's name. "I made the decision then and there to become a paleontologist," he says.

Dino-Mite Discoveries

Since then, Ibrahim has not only achieved his dream, he's become one of the leading paleontologists in the field. He's participated in many important digs, including the hunt for the meat-eating *Spinosaurus*, as well as plant-eating sauropods in Africa. One of his most memorable moments was the discovery of *Alanqa saharica*—a type of pterosaur, or flying reptile that lived during the time of dinosaurs.

Ibrahim and his team made the discovery in the Sahara, where a large river flowed more than 100 million years ago. The river was home to many giant life-forms— and the pterosaur was no exception. Based on the size of the pterosaur's bones, Ibrahim estimates that the animal had a wingspan of about 19.5 feet (6 m). (That's almost twice the size as that of the albatross—the bird with the largest wingspan living today!) More recent finds suggest that *Alanqa* achieved even larger wingspans, making it one of the largest pterosaurs known.

Ibrahim believes that, in spite of its enormous wings, this pterosaur spent much of its time on the ground, where it devoured lizards and small dinosaurs with its slender, beaklike jaws.

Rare Find

Still, that's not the most impressive thing about this finding. Because of the creature's light and flimsy bones, few fossils exist. The vast majority of pterosaur finds have been in Europe, Asia, and the Americas. So Ibrahim's discovery was especially rare because this genus/species of pterosaur, *Alanqa saharica*, is only known from Africa. "All the pterosaur material that has ever been found in Africa could fit on a very small table," he says.

Rewarding Work

Ibrahim's discovery made headlines in the science community—and for him, it was personally rewarding. "I am so inspired by the history of life on our planet and feel it is such a fascinating series of events," he said. "Paleontology is our best tool to understanding this amazing account, and I consider it an absolute privilege to be able to add a few pages to the story."

IBRAHIM EXAMINES
FOSSILS IN THE SAHARA.

Discover a Dinosaur

CONGRATULATIONS! You've discovered a dinosaur skeleton while digging in the badlands of North America. Now there's one thing left to do: Identify it.

You've narrowed down your possibilities to five dinosaurs. Review the facts for each of the following dinosaurs. Then use the clues to identify the fossil you've discovered.

2 You run an analysis of the fossil in your lab to determine its age. It's about 220 million years old.

1 You know that plant-eating dinosaurs (herbivores) had blunt or rounded teeth. Meat-eating dinosaurs (carnivores) had sharp teeth to tear into flesh. So, you take a closer look at your dinosaur's teeth.

THE SUSPECTS

Camarasaurus

LENGTH: 50 to 65 feet (15.2 to 19.8 m) long
DIET: Plants
STANCE: Quadrupedal (walked on four legs)
LIVED: 161 to 146 million years ago

Coelophysis

LENGTH: Less than 10 feet (3 m) long
DIET: Meat
STANCE: Bipedal (walked on two legs)
LIVED: 228 to 200 million years ago

Albertadromeus syntarsus

LENGTH: 5 feet (1.5 m) long
DIET: Plants
STANCE: Bipedal
LIVED: About 77 million years ago

Velociraptor

LENGTH: About 6 feet (1.8 m) long
DIET: Meat
STANCE: Bipedal
LIVED: 99 to 65 million years ago

Ceratosaurus

LENGTH: 15 to 19 feet (4.6 to 5.8 m) long
DIET: Meat
STANCE: Bipedal
LIVED: 161 to 146 million years ago

SO WHAT IS IT?

3 After piecing the skeleton together, you notice the dinosaur's stance. It appears to be bipedal, meaning it walked on two legs.

4 You measure the dinosaur from snout to tail. It's about six feet (1.8 m) long.

Answer: Coelophysis

35

EXPLORE
Peoples and Cultures

DO YOU BLOW OUT CANDLES ON YOUR BIRTHDAY? Do you wear a costume on Halloween or green on St. Patrick's Day? Aside from the fun factor, you might not think much about these customs. But many explorers do. They study people's customs, languages, and beliefs because it gives them a richer understanding of who we are. Why is that important? Many of these cultural practices and beliefs play a role in the way people think and act. Knowing this information helps us to better understand not only other people and societies but ourselves, as well!

MOAI STATUES ON
EASTER ISLAND

HELP WANTED

If you have an interest in exploring the lives of people, consider one of the following careers:

CULTURAL ANTHROPOLOGIST

Responsibilities: Cultural anthropologists are scientists who study past and present cultures, beliefs, practices, languages, values, technologies, economies, and more.

Workplace: Museums, universities, businesses, and hospitals. Cultural anthropologists may also travel to faraway places to study foreign cultures.

What you need: Good social skills, ability to adapt to new things, and a degree in cultural anthropology or a similar field

ARCHAEOLOGIST

Responsibilities: Archaeologists are scientists who study ancient people and their cultures by analyzing old bones and artifacts. Artifacts can be any type of object made by humans, such as tools, weapons, and ornaments. These scientists may go on digs to uncover ancient relics, or they may study them in a lab.

Workplace: Outdoors, museums, universities, labs, and private companies

What you need: A love of travel, camping, and the great outdoors, and a degree in archaeology

BE A ... JOURNALIST!

If you're interested in learning about people, you can start by exploring a festival in your own community. Here's a list of what you'll need and how to do it:

Materials

- Camera or camera phone
- Recording device
- Writing materials
- Internet and/or library

INTI RAYMI FESTIVAL IN PUJILI, ECUADOR

Steps

1. Find a festival you'd like to attend. Grab an adult and go online or head to your local community center to learn about events—such as parades, bazaars, rodeos, or carnivals—in your area. Then mark your calendar.

2. Before you attend your festival, do some research about it. How did the idea for this festival originate? How long has your community held this festival? Who organizes it? How long does it last? What typically happens during this festival?

3. When you attend the festival, take notes about what you see. Are people interacting? What are they wearing? Are people participating in any events?

4. Interview any friends and family members who are at the event. Ask them: Why are you here? Who are you here with? Do you attend this event every year? What's your favorite part of the event? Do you think this event is important for the community? Why or why not?

5. Take photos or video footage of the events and people in attendance. What did you learn?

EPIDEMIOLOGIST

Responsibilities: Epidemiologists are scientists who study the causes of diseases and how they are transmitted to prevent them from spreading or happening in the future. They collect data through observations, interviews, surveys, and blood samples.

Workplace: In a lab or out in the field, where people have been infected by a particular disease

What you need: A willingness to interact with sick patients, good observation skills, and the ability to follow safety precautions are helpful. An advanced degree is required.

LINGUIST

Responsibilities: Linguists are experts who study language. Some linguists may study how different people learn language, others may focus on how a language varies across a specific region, and some study the structure of a specific language.

Workplace: Early childhood to higher-learning organizations, universities, governments, courts of law, and hospitals

What you need: Good listening skills and a degree in linguistics or a related field such as cognitive science, education, anthropology, and computer sciences

Tradition Around the World

OVER THE YEARS, change can cause some traditions to evolve or disappear. For example, ancient Greeks believed in many gods and wrote myths to describe their actions and origins. Most Greeks today might still read these myths but no longer have the same beliefs.

Still, some groups of people have been practicing the same traditions for hundreds—if not thousands—of years. These groups are important to many explorers because of the insight they provide to the past.

Dogon People

WHO: The Dogon people from Mali—a country in Africa—live together in villages that are made of extended family members. Each village is run by the oldest male member. Legend has it that the tribe is descended from four brothers from the west bank of the Niger River.

PRACTICES: The Dogon practice many old rituals—including *dama*, a religious ceremony performed to transport the souls of deceased family members away from the village. During this ceremony, male members of the tribe wear elaborate masks.

Yupik

WHO: The Yupik are a group of people who are native to Siberia; parts of Alaska, U.S.A.; and some islands in the Bering Strait. Historically, the Yupik were a nomadic people. They moved from place to place, wherever food was available.

PRACTICES: In the winter, they had many ceremonies to thank the universe for providing them with food. During these ceremonies, the Yupik performed a *yurak*, or dance, where they wore elaborate costumes. Different types of yurak are still performed today.

Tuareg

WHO: The Tuareg are a seminomadic group of people who are spread across northern Africa. For centuries, the group traveled from place to place, trading items such as gold and rock salt. They also raised animals, such as camels and goats.
PRACTICES: In recent years, droughts and war have forced many Tuareg to settle as farmers or work as seasonal laborers, but many of their customs still remain. The most famous is a blue turban worn by male members of the tribe. The indigo dye used to color the turban often leaves traces on the wearer's hands and face. For this reason, the Tuareg are nicknamed "the blue people."

Navajo

WHO: With a population of 300,000, the Navajo Nation is believed to be the largest Native American tribe. Many members live on reservations in the United States—or land set aside by the government—in Utah, Arizona, and New Mexico. It is believed that the group migrated to the American Southwest from what is now Canada between the years 1100 and 1500.
PRACTICES: Throughout their long history, the Navajo have upheld many of their old traditions, such as the Night Chant ceremony. This ceremony takes place in the late fall or early winter and is believed to cure people who are sick and restore order in the universe. During the ceremony, the Navajo pray, perform dances, and create sand paintings.

EXPLORE NOW!

Tribal masks, like those worn by the Dogon, have a special purpose. For example, animal-like masks are worn for protection, while forest masks promote a great harvest. Think of something that you wish for. Then create your own tribal mask using symbols that represent your wish.

You'll need poster paper, a pencil, a ruler, scissors, construction paper in many colors, paint, glue, markers, and two pieces of string, each measuring one foot (30.5 cm).

> First, think about the shape you want your mask to be.

> Using a pencil, draw the shape on your poster paper. The shape should measure about one foot (30.5 cm) from top to bottom.

> With an adult's supervision, cut out the shape with your scissors. This is your mask.

> Draw two eyes and a mouth on the mask. With a pen or pencil, punch out a hole in each eye to help you see. Then decorate your mask with symbols that represent the thing you wish for.

> Punch a hole on each side of the mask. Then tie one end of a string to the hole on the right side. Tie the other string to the left side.

> Place the mask over your face. Tie the loose ends of string around the back of your head.

INVESTIGATE
Your Family's History

EXPLORERS WHO STUDY PEOPLE keep many journals with information about their subjects. These journals can include observations they've made, interviews, photos, and drawings.

How much do you know about your family's history and traditions? Create your own journal using your family as the subject.

CREATE AN ANCESTRY JOURNAL!

Materials

- Blank journal
- Pencil or pen
- Recording device, such as a digital recorder or cell phone
- Camera
- Tape or paste

Steps

1. Start with an older relative in your family. Write his or her name at the top of the journal page and explain how you are related this person.

2. Take a photo of this person. Print out the image and paste or tape it next to his or her name.

3. Next, interview your subject. Before you begin, be sure to turn on a recording device to capture the conversation.

Then ask your subject their full name, when and where they were born, and questions that will help you learn more about what their lives were and are like. Some examples could be:

→ What are the names of your parents? How would you describe their personalities?

→ Do you have any siblings or any children? If so, what are their names and what are/were they like?

→ What was your favorite holiday growing up? How did you celebrate it?

→ When you were growing up, what were your chores?

→ Did your family have any special traditions or customs? If so, what?

→ What is your favorite family recipe? Your favorite memory?

4. Repeat these steps with other members of your family.

5. Explorers often use the information they gather on people—past and present—to draw conclusions about certain cultures, histories, and traditions. Answer the following questions based on your interviews:

→ What unexpected things did you learn about your family?

→ What traditions or other patterns did you discover?

→ How have your family traditions changed or remained the same over time?

A Trip Around the World

TAKE A TRIP AROUND THE WORLD to discover some amazing artifacts—and learn what they tell us about the past.

Aztec Sun Stone

MEXICO

In 1790, workers repaving the streets of Mexico City's main square discovered an ancient relic just three feet (0.9 m) beneath the ground. The relic, known as the Sun Stone, was carved by the Aztec people who occupied the area during the 15th and 16th centuries. The stone features the sun god Tonatiuh. The stone also shows 20 days, which was the length of an Aztec month.

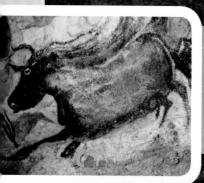

Lascaux Cave Art

FRANCE

In 1940, four boys walked into a cave and discovered one of the earliest examples of prehistoric art; the walls of the Lascaux Cave in Dordogne, France, are covered with paintings that are about 20,000 years old.

EXPLORE NOW!

Archaeologists learn a lot about early humans by studying relics they leave behind. Ask an adult if you can examine the trash. Once you get permission, put on a pair of rubber gloves and head over to your family's trash can. Pretend you are an archaeologist and the trash can is a relic left behind by early humans. What did these humans eat? What jobs did they have? Did they have any pets?

Stone Tools

KENYA

In 2011, archaeologists uncovered a trove of prehistoric stone tools in Kenya, Africa. The tools, which included picks and hand axes, are more than 3.3 million years old! Archaeologists believe that early humans used the tools to crush and cut open food.

Terra-cotta Army

CHINA

People trying to dig a well in northwest China in 1974 didn't quite succeed in tapping water—but they did uncover fragments of a life-size soldier made of clay. Since then, a clay army of 8,000 soldiers, 130 chariots, and 670 horses have been dug up in the area. The soldiers, who sport tunics and armored vests and wear their hair in topknots or caps, provide insight to what China's army wore more than 2,000 years ago.

Valley of the Golden Mummies

EGYPT

When most people think of Egyptian mummies, an image of pharaohs and other royalty comes to mind. But pharaohs weren't the only people who were mummified. The Valley of the Golden Mummies, discovered in 1996 beneath Egypt's Western Desert, contains thousands of mummies from various social classes—including wealthy merchants, members of the middle class, and the poor.

MEET AN EXPLORER

As a boy growing up in Sylvania, Georgia, U.S.A., Lee Berger spent a lot of time searching local fields and riverbanks for Native American artifacts. "It was in these activities that I recognized I had a knack for finding things," says Berger.

Berger eventually took his passion for exploration and turned it into a career. Today, he is a paleoanthropologist. He travels the world searching for and analyzing the bones of ancient humans. These bones tell him what human ancestors looked like and how they evolved.

Major Find

Berger has made many important discoveries. Recently, he worked with a team of researchers to unearth more than 1,550 fossils from a site in South Africa. The fossils belonged to a species that Berger named *Homo naledi*. This human ancestor had a tiny brain and apelike shoulders used for climbing. Because so many bones of this species were discovered, Berger hails the findings as one of the "best known fossil members of our lineage."

Career-Defining Moment

While this finding is impressive, it's not the one that has defined Berger's career. In 2008, Berger and his then nine-year-old son were at a site called Malapa Cave, near Johannesburg, South Africa. Berger's son, Matthew, tripped over a rock and noticed a fossil sticking out of it. They began to dig it out, and eventually discovered that it was a collarbone. "[It was] the very bone I did my Ph.D. thesis on. I will never forget that moment!" he recalls. If that weren't enough, the bone turned out to be two million years old! It had belonged to a species called *Australopithecus sediba*, which was similar to modern-day humans.

Inspiration

With so many great discoveries, Berger couldn't be more thrilled. "The search for early humans is the search for our origins, and that in and of itself is inspiring," he says. "Humans are perhaps the most influential species to ever evolve on this planet and we literally hold the future of this planet's environment in our hands. By understanding our past—where we come from, why we behave the way we do—we can better understand our place on this planet and perhaps become more sensitive to humankind's place in nature."

NO
UNAUTHORIZED
ENTRY

FOSSIL FRAGMENTS
BELONGING TO
HOMO NALEDI

Searching for Lost Cities

MANY ARCHAEOLOGISTS have been on a quest to find ancient cities that vanished over time. These cities were often buried under layers of sediment, which made them difficult to locate. So how do archaeologists get around this problem? With the help of space technology!

Ubar

BACKGROUND: Ubar was a city that was built around 5,000 years ago in present-day Oman, a nation on the Arabian Peninsula. Ubar was a major trade center for frankincense, a resin that was grown nearby. At some point, the city mysteriously vanished. According to some legends, it was swallowed by the desert sand.

DISCOVERY: Based on research conducted by previous explorers, filmmaker Nicholas Clapp was convinced that Ubar was beneath the Rub' al-Khali desert. So, he had NASA researchers use a space shuttle to take images of the desert. The images showed a long road. Using the road as a guide, Clapp and a team of archaeologists were able to uncover more clues to the lost city's location.

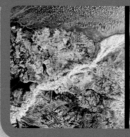

Kingdom in the Sahara

BACKGROUND: The Garamantes were a mysterious group of people who lived in the Sahara more than 1,500 years ago. Experts believe the Garamantes were skilled farmers who dug long tunnels in the ground to access water for their crops. Eventually, the water source ran out—causing the kingdom to fall.

DISCOVERY: In 2011, while examining satellite photographs of an area in southern Libya, researcher David Mattingly and his team noticed more than 100 settlements surrounded by walls. They also saw cemeteries and irrigation systems. Earlier that year, pottery samples found in the same region were confirmed to be the work of the Garamantes, so researchers concluded that these settlements were built by the same people.

Itjtawy

BACKGROUND: About 4,000 years ago, Egyptian pharaoh Amenemhet I established a capital city called Itjtawy. The city was located somewhere on the Egyptian delta—the area where the Nile River empties into the Mediterranean Sea. As new rulers took over, the capital was moved to Thebes, and Itjtawy was abandoned and buried by sediment over time.

DISCOVERY: Using satellite imagery, archaeologist Sarah Parcak was able to see subtle surface changes in an area located near pyramids built by Amenemhet I and his son. Such changes are often caused by building materials that lie beneath the surface. So, Parcak and her team got to work. They began extracting chunks of rock from this area and soon uncovered pottery and stones that were often used in jewelry during the time of Amenemhet I. Parcak believes the site may have been a jeweler's workshop located in Itjtawy.

Crack the Code

NOT ALL CULTURES USE ENGLISH LETTERS while writing. The Chinese use characters called *hanzi*, while Cyrillic script is used in countries such as Russia and Bulgaria.

Throughout history, there have been many different forms of writing, but one of the most famous is ancient Egypt's hieroglyphics, which used pictures instead of letters.

For years, experts had no clue how to read hieroglyphics. They were a mystery until 1822, when a French scholar used an ancient artifact to crack the code. Who was the scholar, and what artifact did he use? To learn the answers, you'll have to use the key to translate the hieroglyphic-inspired messages on the next page.

DID YOU KNOW?

Ancient Egyptians also used hieroglyphics for numbers. For example, a tadpole was used for 100,000, whereas a man with his arms raised represented 1,000,000.

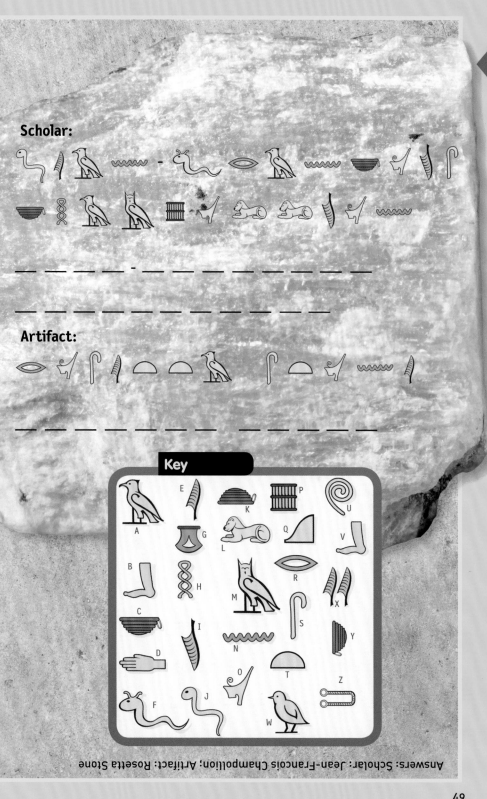

Scholar:

_ _ _ _ _ - _ _ _ _ _ _ _ _

_ _ _ _ _ _ _ _ _ _ _

Artifact:

_ _ _ _ _ _ _ _ _

Key

EXPLORE
Landforms

LANDFORMS ARE NATURAL FEATURES on Earth's surface. They range from continents and islands to mountains and plains. Explorers study the composition of these features and the processes that create them for different reasons. In some cases, the information can lead us to resources that we use every day. For example, minerals that are used to make steel can be found in certain rocks. Knowing which landforms are made of these rocks can help us locate these resources.

In other cases, the information can help save lives. By understanding the processes responsible for these disasters like earthquakes, experts can identify where they can happen—and save lives by helping people prepare.

HELP WANTED

If you are interested in exploring the Earth's terrain, there are many job opportunities for you.

GEOLOGIST

Responsibilities: Geologists are scientists who study the history of our planet to better understand Earth processes and events of the past (including earthquakes, volcanic eruptions, and landslides).

Workplace: Natural resources companies, environmental firms, government agencies, and universities. Geologists also spend time doing fieldwork.

What you need: A degree in geology or a related science such as mineralogy, paleontology, or volcanology

CARTOGRAPHER

Responsibilities: Cartographers are professionals who create and update maps. They must collect, measure, and interpret geographic information.

Workplace: Architecture and engineering firms, governments, and scientific organizations

What you need: A degree in cartography or a related field such as geography or surveying. Courses in computer programming, mathematics, and engineering are also helpful. An attention to detail is a must.

BE A ... CARTOGRAPHER!

To learn more about the different landforms, try this!

Materials

- Computer with an Internet connection
- Pencils, crayons, markers
- Paper

Steps

1 Grab an adult and go online to search for a topographic map of your state. (You may also be able to find a print version at your local library.) A topographic map shows the physical features of land. It can also include structures made by humans, such as dams and roads.

2 Study the map. You should see a color-coded key that's used to indicate the elevation of land, or its height above sea level. Lowlands such as valleys and plains are at one end of the color spectrum, while higher regions, such as mountains, are on the opposite end. Note where these regions appear in your state.

3 Pick another state to investigate. How does its features compare to those of your state?

4 Now that you're familiar with topographic maps, try creating one of your neighborhood. Use drawing materials such as paper, pencils, crayons, and markers. Be sure to include natural features such as forests, lakes, and hills, as well as human-made features such as streets, roads, and parks.

SPELEOLOGIST

Responsibilities: Speleologists are scientists who study, survey, and create maps of caves. They analyze how caves form, the physical features of caves, and the organisms that live there.

Workplace: Government agencies, universities, private geological companies. Speleologists also spend a great deal of time gathering data inside caves.

What you need: A master's degree in a subject such as geology, mineralogy, or biology. Good communication and problem-solving skills, and an ability to remain calm in small, dark spaces will also help.

Fantastic Formations

EACH YEAR, COUNTLESS TOURISTS TRAVEL the world to see and photograph unusual land features, such as crystal caves and stone forests. But for explorers like geologists and speleologists, viewing nature's top attractions isn't enough. Instead, their focus is to understand how these features formed. Take a tour of some of the world's most fantastic formations.

Fairy Chimneys

BACKGROUND: If you happen to be in Cappadocia, Turkey, you'll likely notice strange towering columns across a valley. An old local legend says that these columns were created by fairies, who used the columns as their homes.

HOW THEY FORMED: We know today that these "fairy chimneys" are the result of a volcanic eruption that happened long ago. During the eruption, the volcano spewed out large quantities of ash, which hardened into rock over time. Water and wind slowly wore away the rock, transforming it into these unusual columns.

Cave of Crystals

BACKGROUND: An underground cave in Naica, Mexico, has some of the largest crystals ever discovered. Some measure 36 feet (11 m) long—as tall as a three-story building! The crystals are made from a mineral called gypsum.

HOW THEY FORMED: Scientists believe that the cave once contained scorching hot water that dissolved the gypsum. Over time, the water cooled and deposited the gypsum particles like tiny bricks, forming these mega crystals. The cave's extreme conditions mean it is infrequently visited—and only by experts with special gear.

Grand Canyon

BACKGROUND: The Grand Canyon National Park in Arizona is one of the most famous natural attractions in the United States. It spans 1,904 square miles (4,931 sq km). The canyon is so huge that, according to some reports, the entire population of the world would fit inside with plenty of room to spare!

HOW IT FORMED: The canyon was formed by a combination of natural processes that occurred over time. Within the past 80 million years, Earth's plates—moving slabs of rock that make up the planet's crust—shifted. This caused the ground that the canyon now rests on to lift. The Colorado River, which flowed over the area, carved a gash into the rock, forming the canyon.

Tsingy de Bemaraha

BACKGROUND: In western Madagascar, spiked towers of limestone rock stand 300 feet (91.4 m) above the ground. This enormous stone forest is known as the Tsingy de Bemaraha.

HOW IT FORMED: The "forest" was formed when Earth's shifting plates lifted limestone rock. Over time, groundwater dissolved and cut some of the rock, while heavy rains chiseled the top.

EXPLORE NOW!

To understand how crystals form, create your own crystal garden! You'll need an aluminum pie pan, a sheet of black construction paper, warm water, Epsom salts, a measuring cup, and a tablespoon. To create your crystal garden, do the following:

> Cut a sheet of black construction paper so that it fits neatly in the bottom of the pie pan.

> Pour 1/2 cup (118 mL) warm water into the measuring cup. Add 2 tablespoons (30 g) Epsom salts to the cup and stir.

> Pour the saltwater mixture over the construction paper in the pie pan.

> Place the pan on a windowsill for three days. During this time, the water will evaporate (change from liquid to vapor), and leave behind the salt crystals. These crystal deposits will form a crystal garden.

Forces of Nature

THE GRAND CANYON WAS CREATED largely by a process called erosion. During this process, sand, soil, or rock are moved from one place to another by natural forces such as water, wind, or ice. To demonstrate how erosion works, check out this activity.

ARCHES NATIONAL PARK, UTAH, U.S.A.

DISCOVER EROSION!

Materials

- Pencil
- Scissors
- Paper cup
- A piece of cardboard that measures 1 foot (30 cm) long and 6 inches (15 cm) wide
- Potting soil
- 4 liters (about a gallon) of water
- Large aluminum food tray

Steps

1. Lay the cardboard in the aluminum tray.
2. Cover the cardboard with a thin layer of soil.

3. Then lift one end of the cardboard so that it's one foot (30 cm) off the tray. This represents a steep slope.
4. Have a partner fill a cup with water.

5. Next, have your partner gently pour the cup of water over the raised end of the cardboard until the cup is empty. The water should flow down the slope.

6. Observe the movement of the water. What happens to the dirt?
7. Suppose the slope wasn't so steep. How might that affect the process of erosion? To find out, repeat this activity, but in Step 3 lift one end of the cardboard six inches (15 cm) above the tray. Would water erosion happen faster on a steeper slope or a lower slope?

Answers: Water flows quicker down a steeper slope. The faster the water flows, the more dirt it carries away. So, water erosion would happen faster on a steeper slope.

Antarctica

NOT ALL OF EARTH'S IMPRESSIVE land formations are easy to reach. In 1773, Captain James Cook of England became the first to cross the Antarctic Circle. Since then countless other explorers—including scientists and researchers—have made the trek. So, what can you expect to see on the world's coldest and iciest continent? Plenty!

Mount Erebus

Mount Erebus, located on Ross Island, is the southernmost active volcano in the world. Its most recent eruption began in 1972 and has been ongoing for more than 40 years! Scientists today still study the volcano's gases and lava to understand more about its eruptions.

Ross Ice Shelf

Ice shelves are floating sheets of ice that are connected to a landmass. There are dozens of large ice shelves in Antarctica, but the biggest is Ross Ice Shelf. It spans 600 miles (966 km) in length and measures 3,000 feet (914 m) thick in some parts. In recent years, scientists have been monitoring the Ross Ice Shelf for signs of global warming. Studies have shown that warmer ocean temperatures have been causing the ice shelf to melt from underneath.

DID YOU KNOW?

In August 2010, the temperature in Antarctica dipped to minus 135.8°F (-93.2°C), breaking the record for the coldest temperature ever recorded. The data was captured by a NASA satellite.

Antarctic Desert

Although it's hard to imagine Antarctica without snow and ice, the inner area of the continent is actually a vast desert. It receives only two to four inches (5 to 10 cm) of water—in the form of snow—each year. This makes it one of the world's driest deserts! Some scientists have compared the cold, dry environment to that of Mars. In fact, NASA has tested Mars-bound robots in the Antarctic Desert.

McMurdo Station

McMurdo Station, located on Ross Island, is the largest research center in Antarctica. Here, scientists conduct a variety of experiments. Climatologists use ice samples to study the history of climate. Biologists study the behavior of the continent's wildlife, while astronomers make use of Antarctica's clear sky to study the stars.

South Pole

The South Pole is Earth's southernmost point—and a popular destination for explorers who pose alongside the many flags that surround the area. The flags represent the various countries that signed a treaty stating that Antarctica will be used only for peaceful purposes and scientific research. The Pole is also home to another famous research center—Amundsen-Scott South Pole Station—where many scientists study the atmosphere.

Geographic South Pole

MEET AN EXPLORER

SIMS ASCENDS NYIRAGONGO'S CRATER RIM.

WHO: Kenneth Sims

JOB: Volcanologist

How did you get into geology?

I was a mountain guide for a while. Going to college and studying geology seemed to be the natural next step. I also had some great mentors who inspired me. After college I went to graduate school, where I studied the formation of Earth's core, and did my Ph.D. on Hawaiian volcanoes.

How do your mountain-climbing skills help you with your work?

The skills allow me get to a lot of places in the world where most volcanologists and geologists can't go. Also, as a climber, I've witnessed many accidents, so I've learned to be a cautious person. I think carefully about where I'm at and what I'm doing. This is very important when I'm in a volcano.

When studying a volcano, what do you look for?

I try to determine the amount of time it took for lava to rise and erupt from the volcano, and how long the hardened [form of lava] has been sitting on the surface. Studying this information gives me clues to when this volcano last erupted and how often it erupts. And that information is important because it can be used to predict future eruptions—and warn people who live nearby.

How do you know a volcano won't erupt while you're inside?

If exploring a well-monitored volcano, like Mount Erebus in Antarctica, I know what signs to look for because they've been observed in the past. For example, if a plume of gas goes way up, I know the volcano is becoming more active. We also use technology like GPS monitors and seismometers to measure changes in the Earth. Any changes suggest that an eruption is about to happen.

What volcano are you currently studying?

I'm about to head to Yellowstone National Park. Beneath the surface lies a supervolcano. It erupted 1.4 million years ago, 1 million years ago, and about 600,000 years ago. During the eruptions, it sent ash as far as Texas! Also, the gas—sulfur—that came out of the volcano went through a chemical reaction in the atmosphere. That blocked out sunlight, so crops couldn't grow. And that, in turn, led to famine. It revolutionized life on Earth.

Is a Yellowstone supereruption likely to occur in the near future?

It will happen again, but not in your lifetime. When it does occur, people in the future will know the warning signs, and hopefully, will have the technology to deal with it.

What advice do you have for kids who want to become volcanologists?

Study math and science—and have fun! Working with volcanoes is real science. It involves doing equations and drawing models of what you think might happen. Also, learn to use good judgment. It's a good life skill, and one you need to succeed in a career like this, where there is always an element of risk.

Remarkable Rocks

CAN'T TRAVEL TO THE GRAND CANYON or the Antarctic desert just yet? Don't worry! Bring the great outdoors to you by starting a rock collection in your very own home—there's no better way to brush up on your geology skills. Here's how.

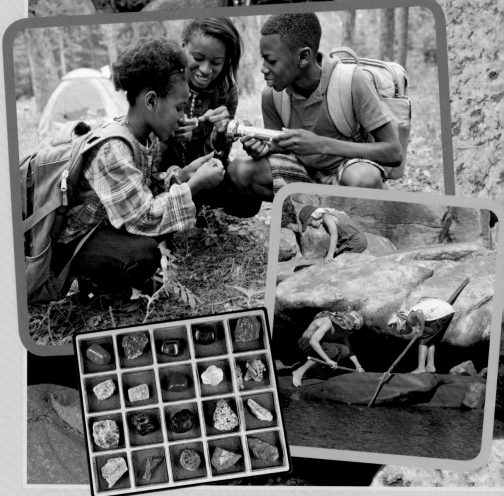

START A ROCKIN' COLLECTION!

Materials

- A bag
- Toilet paper
- Rock guidebook to identify your rocks
- Index cards
- Pen
- A spreadsheet or notebook

Steps

1. Go rock hunting! Start in your backyard or a park. Also, check out rocky areas near rivers, lakes, or beaches. Always bring an adult along!

2. Take notes. Write down the place and date of each rock you've found. Then wrap each sample up in toilet paper so that it doesn't break or chip.

3. Identify your rock. To do this, you'll need to look closely at each sample and use a guidebook to get specific information. But here are the basics: Rocks are naturally occurring solid materials. Almost all rocks are made of minerals, which are solid, nonliving substances that occur in nature.

   There are many different types of rocks, but they can all be grouped into three categories. Check out the chart to the right for details.

4. Label your rock. Now that you've identified your rock, create a label for it. On an index card, write down the type of rock you've discovered, where you found it, and when. Store your index card with its rock.

5. Catalog your rock. A catalog is a record of all the rocks you've collected. As your rock collection grows, having a catalog will help you keep track of all the samples. You can catalog your rocks in a spreadsheet on your computer or by writing the information in a notebook.

6. Make a display case for your rocks. You can use clean egg cartons, extra drawers, or bookshelves to show off your rockin' collection!

TYPES OF ROCKS

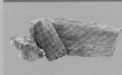

Sedimentary rocks are formed when particles of sand, shells, and other small fragments are deposited by wind or water. These rocks can be identified by their layered look. Examples include limestone, sandstone, and shale.

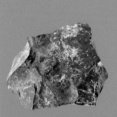

Igneous rocks form when magma, a molten—or partially molten—rock beneath Earth's surface, cools. When igneous rocks cool inside Earth, they're called intrusive rocks. These rocks have visible mineral grains. When the rocks cool above Earth's surface, they are called extrusive rocks. These rocks can have a bubbly or pitted texture. Intrusive examples include gabbro and granite; extrusive examples are basalt, tuff, and scoria.

Metamorphic rocks start out as sedimentary or igneous rocks. Some even start out as different metamorphic rocks. But after being subjected to intense heat and pressure beneath Earth's surface, they change from their original form. When the pressure on the rock is unequal, the resulting rocks often have a striped appearance. But when the pressure is equal, you'll need to identify the minerals that make up the rock to determine the type of rock you've found. Examples include marble, gneiss, quartzite, and slate.

SEA

AHOY, MATEYS!

Are you ready to earn your sea legs? If so, grab your snorkel and a pair of flippers and get ready to explore the ocean, rivers, lakes, and more!

EXPLORE
Underwater Life

THE WORLD'S WATERS are teeming with life. More than 230,000 unique species have been recorded living in the sea alone.

So, who keep tabs on all of these creatures? Scientists, such as oceanographers and marine biologists, spend countless hours diving to extreme depths to study these diverse life-forms.

The information these scientists gather is useful for many reasons. Most importantly, it allows them to detect any factors that may be harming the creatures—such as pollution and a change in water temperature. And because water is essential for human life, problems with Earth's water can mean problems for us. The info also helps us act as the "guardians" of the Earth by protecting the homes of our aquatic friends!

HELP WANTED

If you love the water and can't get enough of animals, one of these marine careers may be for you.

MARINE BIOLOGIST

Responsibilities: Marine biologists are scientists who study organisms that live in the sea. They observe an organism's behavior and the way it interacts with the environment. Some marine biologists specialize in a specific creature, while others may study a specific ecosystem.

Workplace: Marine biologists spend a lot of time underwater, on boats, and in submersibles. They work for governments, museums, universities, and private firms.

What you need: A degree in marine biology or a similar subject, and a love of water and animals

UNDERWATER PHOTOGRAPHER

Responsibilities: Underwater photographers are those who specialize in taking pictures of underwater landscapes, wrecks, and marine life.

Workplace: Underwater, of course! Underwater photographers are often hired by magazine and book publishers, advertising agencies, and scientific research firms.

What you need: A scuba diving certificate and a photography degree

BE A ... MARINE MASTER!

You don't have to be a professional explorer to begin studying underwater life-forms; you can start now! Here's how.

Materials

- Binoculars
- Camera
- Computer tablet or a journal and pen to jot down your observations
- Sunblock
- Sun hat
- Adult supervision

Steps

1 If you're at the beach, look for tide pools. These are small pockets of water left behind after the tide goes out. You might find critters such as starfish, jellyfish, seaweed, hermit crabs, and more. You can also find many shells. Shells are the protective coverings of mollusks, a group of animals without a backbone. Different mollusks have different shells. For example, mussels and oysters have hinged shells, conches and sea slugs have large spiral shells, and creatures called chitons have long, flat shells with overlapping plates. How many of these shells can you find?

2 If you live near a lake or pond, search for wildlife during the spring and summer months. Look for turtles creeping through the grass, frogs resting on lily pads, and insects like dragonflies and water striders.

3 When exploring a river, you may catch a glimpse of a duck or a river otter. Look for plants such as water reeds or lotus plants.

4 Whatever body of water you choose to explore, be sure to snap photos of the organisms you see and take notes about their behavior.

AQUARIST

Responsibilities: Aquarists are professionals who look after fish and other life-forms that are kept in aquariums. They make sure the creatures are fed, maintain water quality and temperatures, clean tanks, repair equipment, and help design exhibits.

Workplace: Aquariums and zoos

What you need: A scuba diving certificate and a degree in marine biology, or a similar field

MARINE TAXONOMIST

Responsibilities: Marine taxonomists are scientists who classify marine life. That means they place organisms into categories based on their structure, origin, and behavior.

Workplace: Taxonomists spend a lot of time in labs. They can work for museums, zoos, aquariums, universities, and companies that are rehabilitating the environment.

What you need: Patience, an eye for detail, and an advanced degree in taxonomy or a similar subject

Water Worlds

JUST AS SOME HABITATS support animals that live on land, others support creatures that live in the water. These aquatic habitats include oceans and seas, ponds and lakes, rivers and streams, and wetlands. Many different animals inhabit each. Dive in to explore some of them.

Oceans and Seas

BACKGROUND: About 97 percent of all the water on Earth contains salt—and the majority of it is found in oceans and seas. Many of the animals that live in these watery regions have mechanisms that allow them to get rid of salt as they take in water.

WHAT LIVES THERE: Most animals, including turtles, sharks, jellyfish, and dolphins, thrive in the upper layers of the water. The well-lit waters make it easy for them to spot food. As you dive deeper, sunlight begins to decrease. So the animals that live here may have large eyes or an ability to produce their own light. These features help them find a meal. In this region you can find strange-looking creatures like lantern fish and anglerfish.

Rivers and Streams

BACKGROUND: Streams are bodies of water that start out as springs or snowmelt and then flow from a higher altitude to a lower one. As they flow, they merge with other streams to form rivers. Generally, the animals that live in these bodies of water have to be able to cling on or swim against the water current.

WHAT LIVES THERE: The middle of a river contains many diverse life-forms. Here, you may find green plants and algae, fish like trout and salmon, and mammals such as river otters and beavers. The mouth of the river can be dark and murky and have less oxygen than other parts of the river. Creatures that live here include fish and shellfish.

Water habitats can be found anywhere—even if you live in a city. Look at a map or go online to determine the body of water nearest you. Then grab an adult and head out to observe the animals that live there.

Make sure to bring along a journal and pen, using the same steps you used when watching animals on the land.

Wetlands

BACKGROUND: A wetland is an area of land that's covered or soaked in water. Sometimes this water comes from nearby lakes, rivers, or springs. In other cases, groundwater is the source of water.

WHAT LIVES THERE: The muddy floors of wetlands are home to a variety of insects, reptiles, and amphibians. You can also expect to find many water-tolerant plants. Depending on which wetland you visit, you might see cattails, lotus, cypress, or duckweed.

Ponds and Lakes

BACKGROUND: Ponds and lakes are bodies of water that are surrounded by land. This means that they usually contain less than one percent salt, making them freshwater habitats.

WHAT LIVES THERE: The edges of ponds and lakes receive plenty of sunlight and contain nutrient-rich sediment. As a result, the shoreline supports the greatest variety of life. Here, you'll find fish, amphibians, insects, rodents, and small organisms called plankton. As you move beyond the shore, the water becomes cooler. Look for algae, small crustaceans, fish, and the larvae of insects near the surface.

DID YOU KNOW?

Frogs shed their skin about once a week.

67

A Closer Look

UNLESS YOU'RE A FISH, viewing life beneath the water's surface can be a bit challenging. To get around this problem, build an underwater viewer. Then use it to explore creatures that live in ponds, lakes, streams, and more.

TADPOLES

FISH AND MINNOWS IN A STREAM

MAKE AN UNDERWATER VIEWER!

Materials

- Empty coffee can
- Can opener
- Duct tape
- Paint and paintbrush
- Plastic wrap
- Heavy-duty rubber band
- Writing materials such as a notepad and pen

Steps

1 Grab an empty coffee can. With the help of an adult, use a can opener to cut out the bottom of the can. Then carefully cover the can's edges with duct tape.

2 Next, use paint and a paintbrush to decorate your can. Place the can aside to dry for a few hours.

3 After the paint has dried, grab a sheet of plastic wrap and cover one end of the can. Secure the plastic wrap to the can with a rubber band.

4 Now you're ready to explore! Take your underwater viewer to a pond, lake, or stream. Stay only at the shallow part of the water—or kneel down on the ground beside the water. Place the part of the viewer that's covered in plastic into the water. Keep still and look through the opposite end of the can.

5 What do you see? Take notes about any plants, fish, insects, or other critters that you observe. Be sure to describe the organisms and what they are doing.

A FISHERIES SCIENTIST RELEASES YOUNG ATLANTIC SALMON INTO A RIVER.

Great Barrier Reef

IF YOU TAKE A DIP IN WARM, tropical waters, you'll likely see colorful structures called coral along the seafloor. There are several coral reef systems around the world, but the most famous is the Great Barrier Reef, located off the coast of Queensland, Australia. Like all coral reefs, the Great Barrier Reef is a bustling ecosystem that is home to a variety of forms of life. Many scientists travel to the reef to study the diverse creatures that live there.

Loggerhead Sea Turtle

Measuring three feet (0.9 m) long, loggerheads are the largest hard-shelled sea turtles in the world. They have powerful jaws which they use to feed on crustaceans as well as jellyfish and sea urchins. From late October to early March, these turtles can be found breeding and nesting along the southern parts of the Great Barrier Reef.

Polyp

Polyps are tube-shaped animals that make hard limestone shells for protection against predators. After the polyps die, their shells are left behind. Over time, these leftover shells build up to form coral reefs.

DID YOU KNOW?

The Great Barrier Reef spans 133,000 square miles (344,500 sq km). It's so large that it can be seen from the moon!

Clownfish

Thanks to their bright orange and white stripes, clownfish are easy to spot. This can be a problem when predators are around. To avoid becoming lunch, clownfish hide in the tentacles of a sea anemone. Sea anemones are a type of polyp that has venomous tentacles. Although clownfish are immune to this venom, its predators are not.

Hammerhead Shark

The hammerhead shark is one of many shark species found in the Great Barrier Reef. Its mallet-shaped head may look strange, but it gives this predator an advantage over others when hunting. Because its eyes are widely spaced, they have a great visual range. This makes it easier for them to spot their favorite snack: stingrays.

EXPLORE NOW!

Many scientific explorers write proposals to companies to sponsor their research. Suppose you are an explorer who wants to plan an expedition to the Great Barrier Reef. What do you want to study? Why? Write a letter to a possible sponsor persuading them why it's so important to conduct this research. Be sure to do some research of your own so you can include specific examples in your letter.

Butterflyfish

Although some butterflyfish come in dull colors, the majority are bright shades of yellow, blue, red, or orange. Their thin bodies allow these fish to move easily through tight passages in the reef system. Butterflyfish can often be seen feeding on polyps, algae, worms, and other small invertebrates.

MEET AN EXPLORER

WHO: Tierney Thys

JOB: Marine biologist

What inspired you to become a marine biologist?

My parents always encouraged a love of the outdoors. I grew up in California, U.S.A., where I went to the beach regularly. Later, I moved to Vermont, where I was nowhere near a beach—but I lived near a stream on the Appalachian Trail. It was incredible! It was this appreciation of the natural world that started it all.

Did you have any mentors along the way?

After college, I planned to go to graduate school but wanted some work experience. Around that time a friend put me in touch with oceanographer Sylvia Earle and engineer Graham Hawkes. At the time, they were looking for volunteers to work on an amazing submersible called Deep Flight. They invited me to join them. It was a great experience and I owe them so much.

So, how did you become aware of the giant sunfish?

One day, while visiting my adviser in graduate school, I noticed a photo of this strange fish on his wall. It seemed odd looking for an open ocean fish because it didn't have a tail! When I expressed interest in the sunfish to my adviser, he suggested that I study them at the Monterey Bay Aquarium, which I did.

What was it like seeing the sunfish live for the first time?

It was magical. These fish are large and have huge eyes. They're also very graceful; you wouldn't think so because of their large size and shape. And some act like puppy dogs! If you have something to feed them, they swim right up to you with their mouth open.

What do the sunfish eat?

Young sunfish will eat a variety of small invertebrates, but as they grow older, they feed mainly on jellyfish.

How do you track sunfish?

I use satellite tags, which I attach to the sunfish below their dorsal fins. I program the tags to take data for a certain period of time. This data includes the fish's location, the temperature it experiences, and the depth to which it dives. When the time I've programmed the satellite tag for is up, it will detach from the fish and float to the surface, where it uploads all the data.

If you could study any other fish, what would it be?

Oh, there are so many! Cephalopods, such as octopi and cuttlefish, are amazing. Mantis shrimp are great. I also would love to swim with a basking shark. I could go on and on!

What advice would you give to a kid who's interested in becoming a marine biologist?

Study your sciences. If your school doesn't offer enough science, go to your local science museum or naturalist center. Or do some exploring online. I would also write to someone you admire. But instead of typing an email, send a handwritten note. It'll definitely get their attention faster!

SUNFISH

Eco-Challenge

EACH YEAR, COUNTLESS SEA CREATURES become victims of overfishing, boating accidents, warming water temperatures, and more. As a result, many of these creatures have experienced a population dip. Thanks to the research collected by marine biologists and other scientists, we at least know which animals are at risk of becoming extinct—and can do something about it. Read on to discover some endangered wildlife and what's being done to help.

Florida Manatee *Trichechus manatus latirostris*

STATUS: Endangered
BACKGROUND: Florida manatees are aquatic mammals that thrive in bodies of warm water from Florida, U.S.A., to Brazil. In recent years, houses and businesses have been built over springs that are homes to these manatees. In addition, collisions with speedboats and other watercraft have taken a toll on the population.
ACTION: Several counties in Florida have reduced their water speed limits. Conservation groups have been establishing protected areas to prevent developers from building in those spots.

Southern Bluefin Tuna *Thunnus maccoyii*

STATUS: Critically endangered
BACKGROUND: At least once a year, the southern bluefin tuna leave their cold-water feeding grounds off the coast of New Zealand and Tasmania and head north to warmer waters of the Indian Ocean to breed and spawn. Unfortunately, few of these fish ever make it out of this area. Most are caught by fishermen. In the past, more than 122 million pounds (55.3 million kg) of southern bluefin tuna have been captured in a single year!
ACTION: Several countries have signed the Convention for the Conservation of Southern Bluefin Tuna. This agreement limits the quantity of fish that can be captured. However, this tuna species still remains endangered.

Blue Whale *Balaenoptera musculus*

STATUS: Endangered

BACKGROUND: The blue whale is the largest known animal to have lived. Until the mid-1900s, whalers often targeted this species, which resulted in a population drop. Recent studies also suggest that global warming may reduce the whale's major food source: krill. With less food to eat, blue whale numbers may continue to drop.

ACTION: In 1966, blue whales became protected worldwide, making it illegal to hunt these animals. In addition, scientists are also closely monitoring the effects of climate change on the species.

Leatherback Turtle *Dermochelys coriacea*

STATUS: Critically endangered (in the Pacific Ocean)

BACKGROUND: Female leatherback turtles bury their eggs in the sand. Unfortunately, some humans dig up these eggs for food. In addition, adult leatherbacks sometimes mistake plastic litter in the ocean for jellyfish—their favorite snack—and end up choking.

ACTION: Some organizations have established protected areas to keep the eggs safe from poachers and have encouraged beach cleanups to prevent plastic and other trash from getting into the water.

Great White Shark *Carcharodon carcharias*

STATUS: Vulnerable

BACKGROUND: Many shark species are experiencing a population drop and the great white is no exception. One reason for the decline is shark finning—a practice in which fishermen cut off a shark's fins, and then throw its body back into the sea. Fishermen sell the fins to restaurants to make soup. Unfortunately, a wounded shark left alive after finning won't survive long.

ACTION: In the United States, the Shark Conservation Act of 2009 made it illegal for fishermen to bring back any shark fins not attached to the shark's body. Conservation groups hope that educating people about the dangers of finning will keep them from ordering the soup.

Bite-Size Information

SHARKS SHED THEIR TEETH many times over a lifetime. Pretend you are a biologist. You've discovered many of these teeth washed up on a beach. It's your job to identify the species each tooth belongs to. Read the descriptions of each of the following sharks. Then use the information to match the shark to its correct tooth.

A

B

C

D

DID YOU KNOW?

There are about 500 known shark species in the world. More than 70 of these species—including those represented in this activity—have seen a population drop in recent years. Human activities, such as fishing, are largely to blame.

EXPLORE NOW!

Just because you're a kid doesn't mean you can't be a marine conservationist. Here's what you can do now to help sharks and other ocean-dwellers:

> Have an adult help you research nonprofit organizations that are doing something to help protect aquatic life. Then hold a bake sale or set up a lemonade stand. Donate the money you make to the organization.

> Participate in beach cleanups. Plastic waste that has been discarded on the sand can be pulled into the ocean by the tides. Marine animals can mistake this plastic for food and then choke on it. So pick up any trash you see.

> Don't buy any products that are made from endangered wildlife. This includes real tortoiseshell accessories, coral necklaces, and shark products.

TIGER SHARK

1 Its teeth have knifelike serrations on one side to help saw through turtle shells.

LEMON SHARK

2 Its teeth are smooth and pointed to help it spear slippery fish.

GREAT WHITE SHARK

3 Its wide teeth have knifelike serrations to cut through large prey, like sea lions.

WHALE SHARK

4 Its teeth are tiny and useless because it feeds on microscopic organisms.

Answers: 1. D, 2. B, 3. A, 4. C

EXPLORE
Underwater Geology

WHEN YOU THINK OF MOUNTAINS, canyons, and volcanoes, you likely think of landforms on dry ground. But these geological features are also found deep beneath the ocean surface.

Understanding underwater geology has many benefits. By exploring these regions, we can learn more about the processes that shape them—like earthquakes—and how to predict them. In addition, many organisms found in these extreme regions have unusual characteristics that help them to survive. Studying these creatures could help lead to scientific breakthroughs in medicine and other areas.

Getting to these remote regions to conduct such investigations can be tricky. But advances in technology have helped scientists collect the data they need to better understand these features and to map the ocean floor.

HELP WANTED

If you have a passion for the oceans and geology, consider one of the following careers:

OCEANOGRAPHER

Responsibilities: An oceanographer is a scientist who studies the ocean. Some oceanographers explore the ocean floor, others study the movements of waves, tides, and currents, while some examine marine life.

Workplace: Research companies, government or environmental agencies, universities

What you need: A degree in oceanography and a good understanding of geology, chemistry, physics and biology

SUBMERSIBLE PILOT

Responsibilities: These pilots prepare underwater vehicles called submersibles for expeditions to the deep waters of the ocean. They also operate the craft and help scientists onboard collect the information they need.

Workplace: These pilots are employed by scientific research companies, and work aboard submersibles and boats.

BE AN ... OCEANOGRAPHER!

Begin your underwater quest—and learn about landforms of the deep—with this map activity.

Steps

1 First, familiarize yourself with these terms: trench, ridge, rift, and abyssal plain. They'll help you understand some common underwater landforms.

2 Check out the map of the ocean floor to the right.

3 Next, answer these questions:

→ What's the longest mountain range on the map?

→ In what body of water is this mountain range located?

→ What continent is located to the west of the Red Sea Rift?

→ The Puerto Rico Trench is located north of which continent?

→ What has a higher elevation: the Mid-Atlantic Ridge or the Demerara Abyssal Plain? Explain.

Answers: Mid-Atlantic Ridge; Atlantic Ocean; Africa; South America; the Mid-Atlantic Ridge because it is a mountain range whereas abyssal plains are flat areas in deep parts of the ocean.

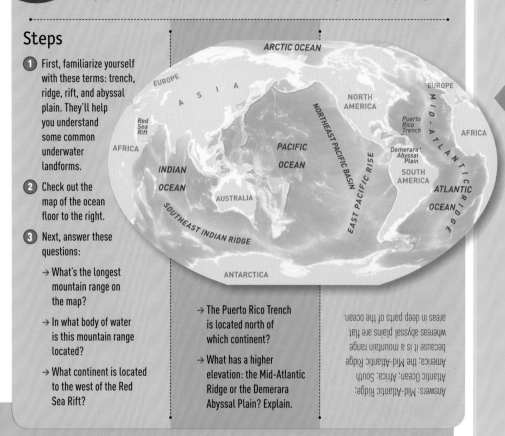

ARCTIC OCEAN

EUROPE

A S I A

Red Sea Rift

AFRICA

INDIAN OCEAN

AUSTRALIA

SOUTHEAST INDIAN RIDGE

ANTARCTICA

NORTH AMERICA

PACIFIC OCEAN

NORTHEAST PACIFIC BASIN

EAST PACIFIC RISE

EUROPE

Puerto Rico Trench

Demerara Abyssal Plain

SOUTH AMERICA

AFRICA

ATLANTIC OCEAN

MID-ATLANTIC RIDGE

What you need: A degree in electronics and the ability to remain calm in small spaces over long periods of time

VOLCANOLOGIST

Responsibilities: A volcanologist is a scientist who studies volcanoes. Some volcanologists specialize in undersea volcanoes and vents.

Workplace: Government agencies, universities, and private companies

What you need: A degree in geology or a similar field. You have to conduct some work aboard a submersible, so you must also feel comfortable being in tight spaces.

HYDROGRAPHER

Responsibilities: A hydrographer is a scientist who measures and describes the physical features of oceans, seas, rivers, lakes, and coastal areas.

Workplace: For a private research company, port or harbor authorities, or national charting companies

What you need: Good math and computer skills and a degree in hydrography, engineering, land surveying, or a similar field

Under the Sea

DID YOU KNOW?

In the deepest part of the ocean, water pressure is so great that it would feel like having 50 jumbo jets piled on you!

ALTHOUGH MOUNT EVEREST and the Grand Canyon are enormous geological features on dry land, they don't hold a candle to those in the deep waters of the ocean. Dive in for a closer look at four landforms and discover what scientists are trying to learn about each.

Mariana Trench

BACKGROUND: The Mariana Trench is a canyon in the Pacific Ocean floor. It is also the deepest place on Earth. With a maximum depth of almost seven miles (11.3 km), it could fit Mount Everest—the world's highest mountain—and still have enough room to spare.

WHAT SCIENTISTS KNOW: Scientists believe that the trench was formed by the movement of Earth's plates—giant slabs of moving rock. As these plates move, they can collide, slide past each other, or pull apart. In the case of the Mariana Trench, one plate slid beneath the other, forming a canyon. Studying the trench has been a challenge for scientists. Only three people have visited the site to date.

Undersea Vents

BACKGROUND: Many volcanoes that form along mid-ocean ridges and plate boundaries produce hot springs called hydrothermal vents.

WHAT SCIENTISTS KNOW: Chimneylike structures along many vents are formed when mineral-rich water heated in the Earth's crust is pushed out of the vents. The water eventually cools and deposits the minerals to form chimneys. Many of the vents release large amounts of carbon dioxide from the chimney structures. This gas causes the water to become more acidic. Scientists are currently studying how this affects organisms that live around these vents.

Tamu Massif

BACKGROUND: Tamu Massif, which spans more than 100,000 square miles (259,000 sq km) isn't just the largest volcano on Earth—it's one of the largest in the solar system. Along with thousands of other volcanoes, it lies beneath the ocean surface.

WHAT SCIENTISTS KNOW: Scientists are still studying how Tamu Massif formed. The popular theory is that magma from deep within the Earth bubbled up to the ocean floor. As the magma poured out, it cooled over time, forming the volcano.

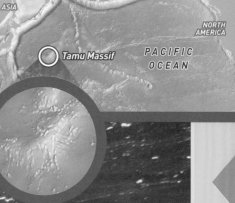

ASIA

NORTH AMERICA

Tamu Massif

PACIFIC OCEAN

Mid-Atlantic Ridge

BACKGROUND: The Mid-Atlantic Ridge is a giant underwater mountain chain that spans 10,000 miles (16,000 km). It begins in the Arctic Ocean and ends near the southern tip of Africa.

WHAT SCIENTISTS KNOW: The ridge formed when two of Earth's plates split apart, causing a rift to develop. The rift filled with hot molten rock called magma, which hardened and over time formed the ridge. In the past 10 years, scientists have discovered various life-forms here—including sea urchins, sponges, and eyeless worms.

EXPLORE NOW!

Water pressure at the deepest parts of the ocean is crushing. Explore how water pressure increases with depth by performing this simple activity:

> Have an adult present to help supervise your experiment.

> Grab an empty milk container.

> Using a pencil or pen, punch three holes in one side of the container: One hole should be near the spout of the container, the second should be in the middle, and the third should be near the bottom.

> Cut a piece of masking tape that's as long as the milk container is tall. Then use the tape to cover the three holes.

> Fill the container with water.

> Place the container in a baking dish and remove the tape.

> Watch the water pour out from the three holes. You should notice that the water shoots out from the bottom hole in a stronger stream than the top and middle holes; that's because the water pressure is greatest here.

81

Discover Acidification

SOME ACIDITY OCCURS NATURALLY, such as in the waters around undersea vents. But pollution and other human by-products can also increase ocean acidity, which can affect shellfish like clams and oysters that use calcium to build their shells. To learn about these effects, try this experiment.

DID YOU KNOW?

Scientists aren't just studying water acidity around underwater vents. They're monitoring this issue in various bodies of water. In recent years, scientists have collected and analyzed samples from the Arctic and Pacific Oceans. The results show an increase in acidity. By making the public aware of this issue now, scientists hope measures can be taken to curb human factors that contribute to the problem.

GIANT CLAMS

TRY THIS *EGGCELLENT* EXPERIMENT!

Materials

- Two large clear cups
- Masking tape
- Marker
- White wine vinegar
- Water
- Plastic gloves
- Two eggshells
- Pen and paper

Steps

1. Grab one cup. Fill it halfway with water. Using masking tape and a marker, create a label for this cup that says "water." Stick it to the cup.

2. Fill your second cup halfway with vinegar. This is your acid. Using masking tape and a marker, create a label for this cup that says "acidic." Stick it to the cup.

3. Put on your plastic gloves. Then grab your eggshells. These are your calcium shells. Place one eggshell in each cup. Be sure to write down what the eggshells look like after you place them in the cups.

4. Place the two cups in a location where they won't be disturbed for 24 hours.

5. After 24 hours, check on your eggshells. Record your observations. Take note of the following:

   → Do you notice a difference between the eggshells in the two cups? If so, describe it.

   → Large amounts of carbon dioxide make water acidic. Based on this experiment, what effect does this have on shellfish?

   → Some human activities, like burning fossil fuels, oil, and natural gas, release carbon dioxide into the atmosphere and water. Based on this experiment, do these activities help or harm ocean life?

Answers: The eggshell in the vinegar should have broken down; the acidity is likely harming the shellfish; these activities harm ocean life.

World's Weirdest Waters

FROM DISAPPEARING LAKES and treacherous seas to red rivers and boiling basins, the world is filled with strange and sometimes dangerous bodies of water. What makes these waters so unusual? Years of exploration have uncovered the truth—and now you can, too.

Lost Lake

OREGON, U.S.A.

During Oregon's wet season you can find Lost Lake in Mount Hood National Forest. But during the summer, something strange happens—the lake vanishes! What's the reason? Scientists have learned that the water drains into two hollow lava tubes created by volcanic eruptions long ago. Rainfall keeps the lake replenished as water drains through the tubes. But in the summer, there is little to no rainfall, so when the water drains out, there's nothing to replace it.

Boiling Lake

DOMINICA

Dominica's Boiling Lake is a well-known hot spring, but you wouldn't want to take a dip there. The lake's temperature ranges from 180°F to 197°F (82°C to 92°C)—and that's just the outer edges. The lake is located in a fumarole, or opening in the Earth's crust, that sits above a magma chamber. The magma heats the water to a blistering boil.

Rio Tinto

SPAIN

Spain's Rio Tinto, which translates to "red river," is a fitting name. The reason for its color is an unfortunate one. For thousands of years, the region surrounding the river has been mined for copper, silver, gold, and iron. Liquid drained from the mines carried these metals to the water, and over time, the iron gave the water a dark red color. However, the color of the water isn't the only effect. The river has a very high acidity, making it unsuitable for many organisms.

Cook Strait

NEW ZEALAND

Cook Strait, a narrow strip of water that separates North and South Islands of New Zealand, is one of the world's roughest bodies of water. What's to blame? The strait lies within the Roaring Forties, a belt of strong winds that circle the globe. The winds blow into the islands' mountain ranges and then flow directly into the strait, turning it into a giant wind tunnel.

cored 2.2 miles

South Pole

Lake Vostok

Lake Vostok

ANTARCTICA

Lake Vostok, which lies 800 miles (1,287 km) from Antarctica's South Pole, is one of the largest lakes in the world. But you'd never guess it because the lake is hidden under two miles (3.2 km) of ice! Scientists believe a unique ecosystem that doesn't rely on sunlight exists in the lake's dark waters.

MEET AN EXPLORER

NAME: Sylvia Earle

JOB: Oceanographer

In 2010, workers on an oil rig had just placed a seal over an underwater oil well they were drilling in the Gulf of Mexico. Suddenly an explosion occurred. The blast opened the well, causing 200 million gallons (760 million L) of oil to gush into the Gulf waters over the course of 87 days. The oil washed over the coastlines and harmed or killed more than 8,000 animals—including birds, sea turtles, fish, and marine mammals.

News of the spill attracted worldwide attention and the fury of conservationists—especially oceanographer Sylvia Earle.

The Ultimate Ocean Expert

Few people truly understand the impact of oil spills on oceans better than Sylvia Earle. This legendary scientist has spent more than 50 years exploring the world's waters.

In 1970, she became one of the first aquanauts when she led a team of four divers to study habitats in the Caribbean Sea while living aboard an underwater craft. In 1979, she broke the record for the world's deepest solo dive when she descended 3,281 feet (1,000 m) in a pressurized suit off the coast of Hawaii. She has also operated and designed numerous submersibles, and she has discovered many marine creatures and unusual landscapes.

A Plea for Help

With a lifetime of deep-sea achievements under her belt, Sylvia Earle is passionate about the world's water—and few things make her angrier than the way humans treat it.

According to Earle, not only were larger animals harmed by the oil spill, but so were plankton. These small organisms, which float in the water, are a source of food for many marine creatures and do a great job of sucking up carbon dioxide—a gas that is largely responsible for global warming.

Earle had the opportunity to voice her concerns in a public hearing before the U.S. Congress. During the hearing Earle explained the importance of the water to the world. "Life in the sea … supports the basic processes that we all take for granted—the water cycle, the oxygen cycle, the carbon cycle, and much more," she said. "With every breath we take, every drop of water we drink, we are dependent on the existence of Earth's living ocean."

SYLVIA EARLE ON AN EXPEDITION
IN THE SARGASSO SEA

Taking Action

Thanks in part to Earle's testimony, oil
drilling in the eastern Gulf has been banned
for seven years. In addition, the government
is trying to update regulations to prevent
similar disasters from happening again.
Meanwhile, organizations like the World
Wildlife Fund (WWF) and the National
Oceanic and Atmospheric Administration
(NOAA) are still monitoring the effects.

Saving Seabirds

TO FIND OUT MORE about the damage that oil spills cause, let's take a closer look at some of the animals that are affected.

Birds use their beaks to preen, or groom, themselves. They arrange their feathers and pick away debris. In the aftermath of an oil spill, seabirds can easily ingest oil caught on their feathers while preening. But this isn't the only danger.

Try out this experiment to discover another way that oil spills can harm seabirds.

DID YOU KNOW?

Puffins are nicknamed "clowns of the sea" for their multicolored bills. The bright colors help the birds attract mates during breeding season, which lasts from spring to summer. In the fall, the birds shed their outer bill, leaving them with a dull-colored beak.

TEST THE EFFECTS OF OIL

Materials

- Two medium-size feathers (can be purchased at a craft store)
- Two large bowls
- Water
- 1 tablespoon (13 g) vegetable shortening
- 2 tablespoons (21 g) cornmeal
- Paper towels
- Watch or timer
- Notepad and pen

Steps

1. Fill each bowl halfway with water.

2. Grab one feather. Using your fingers, coat the feather with the vegetable shortening.

3. Pour the cornmeal on a paper towel. Dip both sides of the greased feather in the cornmeal. This is your "oiled feather."

4. Drop the oiled feather into a bowl of water.

5. Grab the clean feather. Drop it into the other bowl of water.

6. Look closely at the feathers after dropping them into the water. Describe them in your notepad.

7. Leave the feathers alone for about 10 minutes. Then observe them:

   → What do they look like?

   → Did one soak up more water than the other? If so, which one soaked up more water?

   → Which feather seemed to float better?

   → Based on this experiment, how might an oil spill affect birds in the water?

A WESTERN GULL SUFFERS THE AFTERMATH OF AN OIL SPILL.

EXPLORE
People and Water

HUMANS HAVE A RELATIONSHIP with water that has spanned time. We drink it, we cook with it, and we use it to nourish our crops.

But people have also developed other uses for water. Explorers navigated oceans and seas aboard galleons and other sailing vessels to reach faraway lands. Scientists and engineers developed ways to use water as a source of energy.

Today, scientists continue to develop new technologies that use water in innovative ways.

HELP WANTED

If you enjoy helping people and are dedicated to water conservation, one of these careers might be for you:

WASTEWATER ENGINEER

Responsibilities: Wastewater engineers ensure that wastewater and sewage are disposed of safely. They also design and build tools that give communities a constant supply of clean drinking water.

Workplace: Federal and state governments, scientific research companies, engineering companies, and scientific companies.

What you need: Good math, communication, and problem-solving skills; attention to details; and an ability to analyze data. Areas of study include engineering and technology, math, and design.

HYDROLOGIST

Responsibilities: Hydrologists identify and solve water-related problems in society. These problems can include finding water sources for cities and farms and controlling river flooding.

Workplace: Federal and state governments, scientific research companies, engineering companies

What you need: Good problem-solving skills and an ability to interpret data. Students interested in hydrology often study math, physics, and chemistry. Enjoying travel, fieldwork, and wading through water to collect data are also necessary.

BE A ... WATER WHIZ!

Less than one percent of the water on Earth is safe for humans to use. That's not a lot considering there are more than seven billion people on Earth. It's important to conserve and protect the quality of water that is available to us. Many scientists focus their research on identifying and solving water-related problems. Do you have what it takes to do the same?

Materials

- Map
- A library or the Internet
- Writing materials

Steps

1. Grab an adult and head to the library or go online to investigate any water issues that affect your community or state.

2. Start by researching water pollution. Is your community affected by this problem? If so, what's causing the pollution? Sometimes natural factors such as algae blooms and silt from storms are to blame. In other cases, human-related practices, like sewage leaks, wastewater from factories, oil spills, and the use of pesticides, are responsible.

3. Many areas experience dry seasons. But sometimes, these dry periods last much longer than expected. This is called drought—and it can have terrible consequences on crops and wildlife. Is your area affected by drought?

4. Next, look into flooding. If your community encountered this recently, look into reasons why the flooding happened.

Sometimes, excessive rainfall is to blame. But other times, trees and marshes—which can act as barriers to storms—are lacking or have been wiped away. If that's the case, look into reasons why this happened.

5. After you've identified water problems in your area, look into ways that people are trying to solve them. And who knows? You may even come up with your own solutions!

DID YOU KNOW?

Although an adult human might be able to make it for three weeks without food, the average adult cannot survive more than 10 days without water.

HYDROGEOLOGIST

Responsibilities: Hydrogeologists study the quality and flow of groundwater. This is water that's located underground in the soil or rock crevices. Groundwater makes up more than 30 percent of the water that's supplied to homes and businesses.

Workplace: Environmental and engineering firms, research and renewable energy companies, universities, and governments

What you need: Interpreting maps and geographic data, fieldwork, and good communication and problem-solving skills. Areas of study include geology, math, physics, and chemistry.

SOIL AND WATER CONSERVATIONIST

Responsibilities: Soil and water conservationists visit areas that are affected by water erosion and drought in order to come up with solutions.

Workplace: Federal, state, and local governments, utility, construction, and agriculture companies

What you need: Travel, problem-solving skills, and the ability to listen and communicate clearly. Areas of study include natural or physical science, environmental or civil engineering, geography, and economics.

Water Works

WHEN WATER AND TECHNOLOGY MIX, amazing things can happen. Discover some unusual inventions that are making lives easier—without harming the environment.

Clean Water

PROBLEM: Many people who live in impoverished countries do not have access to clean water. Often, they must travel great distances—on foot—to the nearest well or spring. Several pumps that tap into groundwater have been introduced over the years. However, many poor villages cannot afford them.

ACTION: Engineers from Peru's University of Engineering and Technology created a billboard that can produce about 101 quarts (96 L) of clean drinking water each day. How does it work? The billboard's electrically cooled surface condenses nearby air into liquid water. The water is then cleaned by passing through a filter in a process known as reverse-osmosis purification. Eventually, the clean water flows into a storage tank at the base of the billboard and is collected for drinking.

EXPLORE NOW!

Condensation can be used to generate clean water. For an idea of how condensation works, grab two plastic cups, a resealable plastic sandwich bag, and water. Then, follow these steps:

> Fill both cups with cold water.

> Gently place one cup into a resealable plastic sandwich bag. Leave the two cups alone for an hour.

> After an hour, return to check the cups. You should see moisture in the plastic bag. This is condensation.

Energy

PROBLEM: Electricity is often generated by using natural resources such as coal, oil, and natural gas. Unfortunately, these resources are nonrenewable—which means they can't be replaced once they are used up.

ACTION: Scientists are now exploring ways to use ocean waves to generate electricity. One method, designed by scientists in California, U.S.A., would involve placing a giant rubber carpet with cylinders on the seafloor. As waves roll over the carpet, they would create pressure in the cylinders. This pressure would be piped back to shore and converted to energy that could power homes.

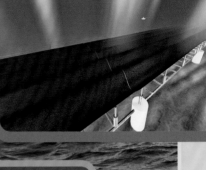

Food Production

PROBLEM: In some parts of the world, a lack of freshwater, fertile soil, and constant temperatures can make growing crops a challenge.

ACTION: To combat this problem, a group of scientists in Italy is exploring an alternative method of farming that involves growing crops underwater! The group has developed seven greenhouses, called biospheres, located off the coast of Italy. There, they grow food like basil, strawberries, and lettuce. The plants get their moisture from condensation that forms inside the glass, while the unchanging water temperature helps make the climate ideal for growing.

Transportation

PROBLEM: Boats big and small have been using the screw propeller to plow through water since the 1800s. Although these propellers make water travel fast and easy, they pose a threat to wildlife. Each year, many dolphins, manatees, and other sea creatures are harmed or killed by the fast-turning blades of these devices.

ACTION: To develop safer forms of transportation, scientists are turning to wildlife for inspiration. The Octopus Siphon Actuator is designed to propel a boat forward by sucking in water and then rapidly expelling it. Scientists based their design on octopi and squid, which rely on a similar method to swim. Best of all? The actuator doesn't use any wildlife-harming blades.

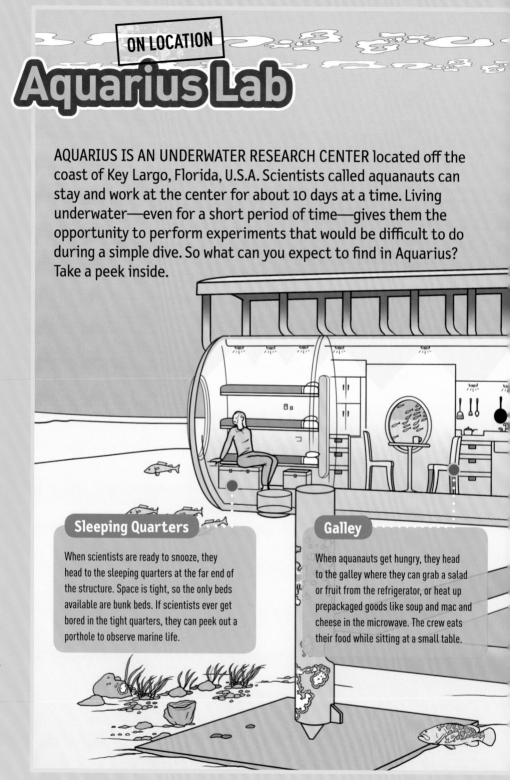

Aquarius Lab

AQUARIUS IS AN UNDERWATER RESEARCH CENTER located off the coast of Key Largo, Florida, U.S.A. Scientists called aquanauts can stay and work at the center for about 10 days at a time. Living underwater—even for a short period of time—gives them the opportunity to perform experiments that would be difficult to do during a simple dive. So what can you expect to find in Aquarius? Take a peek inside.

Sleeping Quarters

When scientists are ready to snooze, they head to the sleeping quarters at the far end of the structure. Space is tight, so the only beds available are bunk beds. If scientists ever get bored in the tight quarters, they can peek out a porthole to observe marine life.

Galley

When aquanauts get hungry, they head to the galley where they can grab a salad or fruit from the refrigerator, or heat up prepackaged goods like soup and mac and cheese in the microwave. The crew eats their food while sitting at a small table.

Workstation

After a dive, aquanauts may want to record their observations at computers set up in a small workstation. In addition to observing sea life, scientists at Aquarius have studied water pollution, the effects of warmer and acidic water on coral reefs, and the properties of light underwater. NASA scientists have used Aquarius as a base while testing out new technologies. The weightless underwater environment mimics similar conditions in space.

EXPLORE NOW!

Suppose you are in charge of the Aquarius research center. You'd like to recruit scientists to join you aboard the center to conduct research. Write a classified ad to attract potential scientists. Your ad should describe the center and explain the type of research that can be done aboard. In addition, you'll want to include some job requirements. (Think about the characteristics a person would need to live underwater for 10 days.)

Buoy

Scientists are able to live in this underwater habitat thanks largely to a buoy on the ocean surface. The buoy supplies air and electricity to the lab below. It also contains radios that allow aquanauts to communicate with mission control, which is located on land.

The Wet Porch

Divers enter Aquarius through a "wet porch" located under the structure. Once inside the vessel, they can store their dive equipment in this area, and take a freshwater shower.

MEET AN EXPLORER

WHO: Feliciano dos Santos

JOB: Musician and Activist

What do music and clean water have in common? A lot, if you ask Feliciano dos Santos. For about 20 years, this musician has been educating people about the importance of clean water through the power of song.

Danger in the Water

Santos was born in the Niassa Province of Mozambique, a country in southeastern Africa. Here, diseases like hepatitis A and typhoid are prevalent, and the average life expectancy is only 42 years.

Several factors are to blame, but poor sanitary practices and a lack of clean water are perhaps the biggest culprits. To get water for drinking and household needs, people must go to a river, where the water is unprotected. That means anyone can legally dump pollutants into it. In addition, less than 3 percent of all homes have plumbing, so people must dispose of human waste outdoors. The issue becomes a big problem when people fail to follow sanitary practices—like washing hands. As a result, harmful bacteria and viruses are spread easily from person to person.

Making a Difference

Dos Santos knows the consequences of these factors firsthand. When he was a child, he contracted a deadly disease called polio. The disease is spread by contaminated food and water. Dos Santos was fortunate to survive the disease and vowed to bring change to Niassa and other parts of Mozambique.

Attracted to music, dos Santos formed a band in the 1990s called Massukos—which he has used to educate people. The band sings songs about the importance of washing hands, boiling water, and building latrines in the tribal language of Niassa. Many people—most importantly, those who live in areas where these problems are rampant—were inspired by the music.

Still, dos Santos wanted to do more. So he formed a nonprofit group called Estamos, which works directly with the villagers. The group has convinced people to install thousands of environmentally friendly latrines that won't contaminate drinking water. As a result, sanitation has been improved and diseases have been reduced throughout the region.

"I don't want to see anyone else go through what I did because of unclean water," says dos Santos.

CHILDREN WASH THEIR HANDS TO HELP PREVENT
DISEASE DURING GLOBAL HANDWASHING DAY IN KENYA.

Testing the Waters

LACK OF CLEAN WATER is a major problem in many parts of the world. One way to clean water is by using a device to filter, or remove, impurities. To learn how a water filter works, try building your own.

A WOMAN PUMPS WATER IN NEW DELHI, INDIA.

MAKE A WATER FILTER!

Materials

- A large plastic bottle (cut in half by an adult)
- Paper towels
- ½ cup (113 g) gravel
- ½ cup (113 g) sand
- A coffee filter
- Large measuring cup
- 2 cups (470 mL) water
- 1 tablespoon (15 mL) cooking oil
- Tiny bits of Styrofoam
- Pieces of paper cut up into strips

Steps

1. Have an adult poke a hole in the cap of the water bottle. Then secure the cap to the bottle.

2. Take the top half of the bottle and place it upside down, inside the bottom half of the bottle.

3. Place a coffee filter inside the top half of the bottle. The filter should lie against the cap.

4. Pour the sand on top of the filter.

5. Complete your homemade water filter by pouring the gravel on top of the sand.

6. In a large measuring cup, add the water, cooking oil, Styrofoam, and paper strips. This is your dirty water.

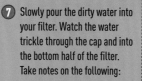

7. Slowly pour the dirty water into your filter. Watch the water trickle through the cap and into the bottom half of the filter. Take notes on the following:

   → How did the water look before you poured it into the filter?

   → Was the water's appearance different after you poured it into the filter? If so, how?

   → In which part of the filter were the different pollutants caught?

Note: Although this filter helps eliminate some pollutants, it does not filter out bacteria, so it should not be used for drinking water.

EXPLORE
Water and the Past

SOME ARCHAEOLOGISTS AND OTHER SCIENTISTS explore underwater to find relics from the past. In the past 30 years alone, these experts have discovered pirate and wartime ships, weapons such as canons and swords, and an assortment of riches that include jewels, gold and silver coins, and more.

Discovering such treasures can be a huge thrill for scientific explorers—mainly because of the wealth of information they offer. By studying these relics, scientists can learn more about human culture and behaviors—and sometimes even solve mysteries related to how these items ended up underwater in the first place.

HELP WANTED

If you have a passion for water and exploring the past, you might consider one of the following careers:

UNDERWATER ARCHAEOLOGIST

Responsibilities: Underwater archaeologists go on dives to find artifacts and other remains left by people. They study these finds to learn about the past.

Workplace: Governments, universities, and scientific organizations

What you need: A scuba diving certificate, a love of history, and a degree in archaeology

OBJECT CONSERVATOR

Responsibilities: Conservators are people who repair and preserve objects from the past.

Workplace: Museums, governments, scientific organizations

What you need: A degree in art conservation or history. Courses in chemistry, the humanities—such as art, archaeology, anthropology, and architecture—and studio art

BE AN ... UNDERWATER DETECTIVE!

According to some studies, only 5 percent of the ocean has been explored. Imagine how many shipwrecks and other relics are waiting to be discovered! So how do you begin looking for these historical treasures? Well, it helps to have sonar equipment and a submersible to scan the ocean floor. But you can do other things to get started.

Materials

- The Internet
- Library
- Map

Steps

1. Many underwater explorers are history buffs. They read about ships and treasures lost at sea. Knowing when and where the ship was lost could provide important clues about the location. (You'll read more about this later.) With that in mind, grab an adult and head to the library or go online to begin your investigation. Look for boats that were lost and never found. Where were they? And when did the shipwreck happen? What was the cause? Plot your clues on a map.

2. Since you probably don't own a submersible, look for science organizations that actually do underwater exploration, such as Woods Hole Oceanographic Institution (WHOI) or the National Oceanic and Atmospheric Administration (NOAA). Ask an adult to help you email the organization to find out if there are any volunteer opportunities.

ROV PILOT OR TECHNICIAN

Responsibilities: ROV (remote-operated vehicle) pilots navigate and maintain underwater robots that capture images and other data in the ocean. These robots can be used to locate shipwrecks on the ocean floor.

Workplace: Scientific organizations

What you need: A passion for electronics and a degree in engineering, biology, or earth sciences

HISTORIAN

Responsibilities: Historians are experts who analyze written accounts about the past, government documents, film footage, and recordings. They piece together the information from these sources to get a better understanding of what life was like.

Workplace: Universities and government institutions, and also as consultants for television and movie productions

What you need: A college degree, patience, writing and puzzle-solving skills

Underwater Discoveries

WHEN MOST PEOPLE THINK of underwater discoveries, they think of shipwrecks. But over the years explorers have made other fantastic finds—including forests, temples, animal fossils, and even mummies.

Bog Mummies

BACKGROUND: Across northern Europe, more than 2,000 ancient bodies have been discovered in swamplike areas called peat bogs. The most famous discovery is Tollund Man, discovered in Denmark in 1950.

WHAT WE KNOW: Scientists concluded that Tollund Man was more than 2,000 years old and was likely a human sacrifice! The reason his body is preserved is because the organisms that cause decay—bacteria and fungi—are not present in the bog. Why not? A moss in peat bogs shuts out oxygen, which bacteria and fungi need to survive. In addition, bog water contains chemicals that make the mummies' skin tough and long lasting.

PEAT

Animal Fossils

BACKGROUND: While exploring an underwater cave off the coast of Madagascar, divers discovered a graveyard of animals that includes lemurs the size of gorillas and horned crocodiles. The bones were well preserved and are more than 2,000 years old.

WHAT WE KNOW: The animals may have been washed away in a flood. Because underwater caves don't get a lot of foot traffic, the bones have not been disturbed—which explains their excellent condition. On land, the bones would likely have been eaten or crushed by stampeding animals or other forces of nature.

Prehistoric Forests

BACKGROUND: A diver named Dawn Watson was exploring the water near Norfolk, England, when she spotted giant structures sprawled across the seafloor. At first, Watson thought it was a shipwreck, but when she went in for a closer look, she realized the structures were giant tree trunks and branches.

WHAT WE KNOW: According to scientists the trees are the remains of a 10,000-year-old oak forest. The forest was part of Doggerland, a giant landmass that extended from present-day England to Germany. Scientists believe the trees were toppled over by a tsunami that flooded the region 8,000 years ago.

Ancient Temples

BACKGROUND: In December 2004, a tsunami wreaked havoc along the Indian Ocean. Some objects that had been underwater suddenly surfaced. In India, a granite lion monument and parts of a wall that depict elephant, lion, and horse carvings became visible.

WHAT WE KNOW: Archaeologists believe that the wall was part of a temple built between the first century B.C. and the second century A.D. The animal engravings and lion structure may have been added hundreds of years later. As for how they were revealed in the water? The same way they ended up there: A tsunami triggered by a giant earthquake was most likely to blame.

EXPLORE NOW!

Suppose you are a historian helping scientists who are examining the Tollund Man. Based on their findings, you know that he lived in the fourth century B.C. in what is present-day Denmark. With the help of an adult, research what life was like for people who lived there during that time to help scientists get a better idea of who Tollund Man was.

103

Shipwrecks

SHIPS SINK FOR VARIOUS REASONS. Many are toppled over by stormy waters and rogue waves, some crash into rocks or icebergs, while others are destroyed during wars. Experts estimate that more than three million shipwrecks are lying on ocean floors around the world! Check out some of the most famous wrecks of all time.

Titanic

NEAR NOVA SCOTIA, CANADA
When the *Titanic* struck an iceberg in 1912, it took less than three hours for the giant ocean liner to sink. About 1,500 people died—making it one of the biggest disasters of its time. The wreck wasn't found until 1985, when oceanographers Robert Ballard and Jean-Louis Michel discovered it by towing an underwater camera across the ocean floor. Since then, scientists have studied parts of the ship that have been brought to the surface.

Whydah Gally

NEAR CAPE COD, MASSACHUSETTS, U.S.A.
Captain Sam Bellamy was a notorious pirate who commanded a ship called the *Whydah Gally*. In 1717, the ship was smashed against large rocks, and everyone aboard perished. For years, the wreck remained hidden under ocean sand. But in 1984, Barry Clifford, who had dreamed of finding the wreck since he was a kid, achieved his goal. Using a funnel and the propellers of his own boat as a giant fan, he was able to whip up ocean sands and uncover the wreck. Since then, many artifacts have been uncovered—including a 2,500-pound (1,134-kg) cannon that would have required four people to operate.

Lusitania

NEAR COUNTY CORK, IRELAND

In 1915, World War I was under way, and ships were under enemy fire. Officials tried to warn the crew of the *Lusitania*, a giant passenger ship, but the crew pressed on. As the ship sailed past Ireland, a torpedo fired by a German submarine, along with a mysterious explosion aboard the ship, sank the *Lusitania*. The wreck was located in 1935, and since then numerous explorers have examined the boat, hoping to discover the reason for the mysterious blast. In 1993, Robert Ballard, who discovered the *Titanic* wreck, concluded that it was caused by a coal-dust explosion.

A CREW RECOVERS ARTIFACTS FROM THE WRECK OF THE *QUEEN ANNE'S REVENGE*.

Queen Anne's Revenge

NEAR NORTH CAROLINA, U.S.A.

During the 18th century, Blackbeard and his pirate crew terrorized ships while sailing aboard the *Queen Anne's Revenge*. But in 1718, the tides turned for the notorious pirate. His ship ran aground and sank in shallow waters in North Carolina, where it remained for nearly 300 years. Divers discovered the wreckage in 1996, and since then archaeologists have uncovered thousands of artifacts from the ship. Among the artifacts were syringes and other medical equipment likely used by ship surgeons to treat wounds and diseases.

EXPLORE NOW!

Saltwater shipwrecks are often more corroded than those in freshwater. To see this in action, have an adult help you grab two cups, water, salt, four nails, and a marker. Then try this experiment:

> Fill each cup with water.

> Add 1 tablespoon (13 g) salt into a cup and stir. Using a marker, write the word "saltwater" on this cup.

> Write the word "freshwater" on the cup that has no salt.

> Drop two nails into each cup. Then set the cups aside for 24 hours. When the time is up, examine the nails in each cup. Which has more rust?

NOTE: Save these nails for the activity at the end of this chapter.

MEET AN EXPLORER

WHO: Mark Polzer

JOB: Nautical archaeologist

What inspired you to become a nautical archaeologist?

I lived abroad when growing up, including six years in Libya. Libya was inhabited at various times by ancient Phoenician, Greek, and Roman settlers and today boasts magnificent ruins. I got to explore these ruins with my family, and we also spent many holidays touring other ancient sites …

My father also taught me to scuba dive. On occasion we would find broken pottery strewn across the reefs fronting our beach, likely the remains of ancient shipwrecks.

What courses did you take to help prepare you for your career?

Since my main interest is the ancient Mediterranean, I took courses in Greek, Roman, and Near Eastern history. [I also] took courses in artifact conservation and archaeological chemistry so I can care for and analyze the objects that I find. Finally, since I specialize in nautical archaeology, I took courses in wooden shipbuilding, [ancient] seafaring, and the research and reconstruction of ships.

How do you locate a shipwreck?

Shipwrecks are located in all sorts of ways. Most have been discovered accidentally. The last site that I excavated, a Phoenician shipwreck at Bajo de la Campana, Spain, was found by chance in the 1950s by commercial divers while they were salvaging scrap iron.

In other circumstances, archaeologists use an array of technologies to conduct remote sensing surveys, so called because they use machines and instruments to do the actual searching and recording, while a technician operates them from the surface.

What did you uncover from the Phoenician shipwreck?

Almost all of the objects we uncovered were items that were to be traded at the ship's destination. We recovered an astonishing variety of goods: approximately 60 elephant tusks from North Africa; minerals and raw metals (lead, copper, and tin) most likely mined in Spain; pieces of amber (the fossilized resin of ancient trees) from northern Europe; many different types of pottery; and an assortment of luxury pieces probably intended for an important local ruler or chieftain.

What do these relics tell us about the Phoenicians?

The pottery and raw materials we found, the elephant ivory, lead, copper, tin, and amber, are particularly interesting because they tell us about Phoenician trade networks and economies. This, in turn, helps us to learn about these ancient peoples and the world in which they lived.

What's the biggest challenge for you when exploring an underwater wreck?

Every shipwreck (or land site) that I have explored has presented me with different sets of challenges. For some, it was the depth of the site that was most limiting. The deeper the site, the shorter the amount of time a diver can spend underwater working on it, and the greater the risk of decompression sickness (also known as the bends). On the other hand, the Phoenician shipwreck site at Bajo de la Campana was shallow (49 to 197 feet [15 to 60 m]), so our dive times were quite generous. The challenge there was that the site was covered with large boulders and rock debris, which we had to remove at the start of each field season before we could begin excavating.

What advice would you give to a kid who dreams of doing what you do?

Most importantly, believe in yourself and follow your dream. Like any worthwhile pursuit in life, archaeology requires hard work, perseverance, and a good deal of study. Whether watching an archaeological documentary on television, visiting an ancient site, taking in a museum exhibition, or attending an archaeological lecture, never stop learning.

Ruinous Rust

ARCHAEOLOGISTS MAY USE A VARIETY of ways to clean rusted artifacts. Sometimes, they chip the rust off. Other times, they use chemicals. Is there an advantage to using one method over the other? Clean your artifacts to find out.

BE AN ARCHAEOLOGIST!

Materials

- Two rusted nails from the Explore Now! activity on page 105
- Plastic cup
- ½ cup (120 mL) white wine vinegar
- Paper towel
- Toothpick
- Measuring cup
- Notepad and pen
- Adult supervision

Steps

1. Pour the vinegar into the plastic cup. This is your chemical.

2. Carefully place one rusted nail into the cup. On your notepad, describe the appearance of the nail in the cup. Then place the cup aside for 24 hours.

3. Next, place a paper towel on a table. Then place the second rusted nail on the paper towel. Using a toothpick, gently scrape the rust off your second artifact. But be careful! It's an old artifact.

4. After you are done, describe on your notepad the process and the amount of rust you were able to remove.

5. After 24 hours, remove the artifact from the cup. Describe the artifact in your notepad. Note the following:

   → How did the vinegar affect the nail?

   → Which method removed more rust: hand-chipping or vinegar submersion?

   → Why do you think archaeologists would choose to clean some artifacts with chemicals and others by chipping off the rust?

SKY

READY FOR TAKEOFF?

The sky's the limit—and you're about to find out why. Grab a spaceship (or a telescope) and get ready to explore the clouds, the stars, and everything in between.

EXPLORE
Wildlife in Flight

UP UNTIL NOW, you've learned about explorers who seek out animals that live on land or in bodies of water. But some animal pros study the physical characteristics and behaviors of birds, insects, and other high-fliers.

Some explorers use the information they learn to protect these creatures. Other explorers observe these creatures to understand their mechanics. Using this information, they develop aircraft and other technologies that mimic the animals' flight.

You'll get a bird's-eye view of these innovations and more on the following pages.

GREAT HORNBILL

HELP WANTED

If you have a thing for winged creatures, consider one of the following careers:

ORNITHOLOGIST

Responsibilities: Ornithologists are scientists who study birds by monitoring their activities and analyzing the data they've collected.

Workplace: Universities, museums, research companies, governments, and wildlife and environmental organizations

What you need: Patience, a love of birds, and an advanced degree in ornithology or other similar life science

ENTOMOLOGIST

Responsibilities: Entomologists are scientists who study the life cycles and behaviors of insects.

Workplace: Museums, governments, and universities

What you need: Patience, a love of insects and bugs, and a degree in entomology or a relevant field

BE A ... BIRD BUFF!

Begin your exploration of airborne creatures with the following tips. The steps may be written with birds in mind, but you can use them to observe any creature that takes flight.

Materials

- Binoculars
- Notebook and pen
- Field guide (to help identify your birds)

Steps

1. With an adult, go to a local library or nature center and ask about bird walks. Otherwise, go to an area with plenty of trees, such as a park or nature reserve.

2. When you're ready to begin your observations, try not to stand out too much, or you might frighten away the birds. Don't speak loudly, and wear clothes that will help you blend in with the environment.

3. Listen closely for any sounds. When you hear a bird, try to find it with your naked eye. Once you've honed in on the critter, grab your binoculars without taking your eyes off the bird. Bring the binoculars slowly to your eyes for a close look.

4. As you observe the bird, ask yourself these questions: What is it doing? Is it building a nest? Is it feeding its young? Or is it pecking a tree or perched on a branch? What does the bird look like? Is there anything unusual about it?

5. After you've observed the bird, record your observations. If you didn't recognize the bird, you can use the information you recorded to find the bird in your field guide.

CAUTION!

Do not disturb any nesting birds or bird nests. If you find a baby bird away from its nest, don't touch it. Its mother is likely nearby. If that isn't the case, contact an animal control and welfare center, or your local Audubon Society. This is an organization that specializes in bird conservation.

MECHANICAL ENGINEER

Responsibilities: Mechanical engineers are people who study how things work. Then they design and develop new devices based on their research. Some mechanical engineers study the behavior and physical characteristics of wildlife, including birds, to develop products that improve human life.

Workplace: Universities, research companies, and governments

What you need: Curiosity, good problem-solving skills, and an advanced degree in mechanical engineering, biomechanics, or related subjects

CHIROPTEROLOGIST

Responsibilities: Chiropterologists are scientists who study bats. They often observe bats in their native habitats to learn more about their behavior, and they also study bat biology in labs.

Workplace: Universities, museums, research companies, and conservation groups

What you need: A love of bats and an ability to remain calm in dark places. You'll also need a degree in a relevant life science such as biology or zoology, and classes in chiropterology.

Frequent Fliers

THANKS TO SCIENTISTS who are using video footage, tracking devices, and high-speed x-ray cameras, we now have a better understanding of some of nature's more unusual frequent fliers.

Wandering Albatross *Diomedea exulans*

BACKGROUND: Weighing up to 25 pounds (11.3 kg), the wandering albatross is a hefty bird. Yet it can fly for hours without flapping its wings. What's this seabird's secret?

WHAT WE KNOW: The albatross uses an unusual up-and-down flying pattern. The bird swoops downward, gaining momentum as it glides. It then uses this momentum to propel itself upward. In addition, the bird's long, slender wings reduce drag, a force that slows movement. These factors help the albatross travel long distances without much effort.

Lesser Galago *Galago*

BACKGROUND: Lesser galagos, or bush babies, don't exactly fly—they travel in leaps and bounds. These small furry mammals can cover up to eight feet (2.5 m) in a single leap. That's the equivalent of a human jumping two double-decker buses!

WHAT WE KNOW: Their jumping abilities have a lot to do with the springy tendons in their legs. When a bush baby lands, these tendons stretch like rubber bands and store some of the energy from their previous jump. The tendons then snap back and release this energy—propelling the bush baby as it takes a giant leap forward.

Ruby-Throated Hummingbird *Archilochus colubris*

BACKGROUND: To fly, birds need to produce an upward force called lift. Most birds do this by flapping their wings down. But hummingbirds can generate lift during an upward stroke as well. How?

WHAT WE KNOW: The secret is in the wrist! Before flapping upward, hummingbirds twist their wrists, causing their wings to flip. During these movements, the bird's chest muscles contract to deliver extra power to each stroke. As a result, hummingbirds can beat their wings more than 53 times a second.

DID YOU KNOW?

Hummingbirds get their name because their speedy wings make a humming sound as they flap.

Paradise Tree Snake *Chrysopelea paradisi*

BACKGROUND: Snakes can slither, swim, and sidewind. And some can even fly! Some so-called flying snakes, like the paradise snake, glide up to 330 feet (100 m) in the air!

WHAT WE KNOW: The snake prepares for takeoff by slithering to the end of a branch. From there, it dangles in a J-shape and then uses its muscles to fling its body up and away from the branch. Once airborne, it forms the letter S and flattens its body, transforming itself into a flying wing.

EXPLORE NOW!

To demonstrate how hummingbirds flap their wings, put your arms to your side. Then, keeping your elbows against your hips, flap your forearms backward and forward.

Flying Squirrel *Pteromyini*

BACKGROUND: When a flying squirrel jumps out of a tree, it doesn't drop like a rock. Instead, it glides to the ground! The squirrel can cover 150 feet (45.7 m) in just one glide.

WHAT WE KNOW: The squirrel begins its descent by spreading the furry folds of skin located between its wrists and ankles. The skin acts like a parachute, allowing the squirrel to glide instead of fall. A cartilage rod attached to the squirrel's wrist helps the animal steer, while its tail keeps it stable during flight.

Get Gliding

SOME ENGINEERS ARE SO AMAZED by the way flying creatures are able to move almost effortlessly across the sky that they design aircraft modeled after these animals. Suppose you are a mechanical engineer. Can you build a glider that's modeled after a flying squirrel?

AN EXPERIMENTAL GLIDER IN 1891

BUILD A FANTASTIC FLIER!

Materials

- Piece of paper

Steps

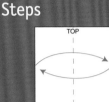

1 Fold a piece of paper in half lengthwise. Press the crease with your thumb for a better fold. Then open the paper back up.

2 Fold the upper corners of the paper in toward the crease you created in Step 1. The top of your paper should now look like a triangle.

3 Fold the triangle down toward the bottom half of the paper. Your paper should now resemble an envelope.

4 Take an inch (2.5 cm) of the tip of the triangle and fold it up to make a crease. Then unfold it. The crease you just created should cut across the crease you made in Step 1. The two creases should form a cross.

5 Take the upper corners of the envelope shape and fold them inward until they meet in the center of the cross.

6 Fold the tip of the triangle up so that it covers the part where the two corners from Step 5 meet.

7 Fold the paper back along the lengthwise crease.

8 On one side, create a top wing by folding the paper downward. The top of the wing should be parallel with the bottom of the paper.

9 Repeat Step 8 with the opposite side of the glider.

10 Take your glider out for a test drive! Hold your glider by pinching the two sides of the small triangle. Throw your glider forward. Watch your glider as it descends to the ground. Write down your observations.

11 After a few test runs, unfold the wings you created in Steps 8 and 9. Then repeat Step 10. Take note of the following:

→ Did the flight pattern change in Step 11?

→ Based on these observations, how does a flying squirrel's outstretched skin help it descend to the ground? How would this information help you build a flying machine?

Answers: Answers may vary, but most kids will notice that the glider had a smooth, even descent in Step 10, but took a nosedive in Step 11.

117

Migrations

MANY BIRDS, INSECTS, AND WINGED MAMMALS take to the skies each year, seeking sources of food, breeding grounds, and warmer climates. Their destinations have not always been known. Thanks to tracking devices and tagging, scientists have been able to discover where exactly these creatures go and why.

Arctic Tern *Sterna paradisaea*

ARCTIC CIRCLE TO ANTARCTICA
The arctic tern weighs only four ounces (113 g), but don't let this lightweight fool you. Twice a year, the bird makes an epic trek from one end of the Earth to the other. From May through September the tern can be found in the Arctic. But as winter approaches, temperatures drop and food becomes scarce. So the birds head to Antarctica, where they remain until February. Each leg of the journey is about 22,000 miles (35,400 km)!

Globe Skimmer *Pantala flavescens*

INDIA TO EAST AFRICA
The globe skimmer is a dragonfly species that breeds in rainwater pools. Naturally, it enjoys spending time in India during the monsoon season, when the country experiences heavy rainfall. When the rain moves on to East Africa in the early fall, so do the globe skimmers. The insects continue to follow the rains to southern Africa and back to India. The trip spans 11,000 miles (17,700 km), making this the longest known migration for an insect.

Bar-Tailed Godwit *Limosa lapponica*

ALASKA, U.S.A., TO NEW ZEALAND

Before they head south for the winter, bar-tailed godwits get so plump they look like flying softballs. They need the extra bulk to make their epic migration. In autumn, the birds fly from Alaska to New Zealand without landing to eat or drink. Scientists tracked one bird that traveled 7,145 miles (11,500 km) nonstop in nine days! That's the longest nonstop flight for any bird.

Mexican Free-Tailed Bats *Tadarida brasiliensis mexicana*

SOUTHWESTERN UNITED STATES TO MEXICO

Each spring, millions of free-tailed bats leave their winter homes in Mexico and head to southwestern parts of the United States, where they find homes in caves and mines. Here, the bats give birth to live pups. The mother bats feed their young until they are old enough to hunt. By winter, the pups have grown and the bats return to Mexico.

Monarch Butterfly *Danaus plexippus*

CANADA AND UNITED STATES TO MEXICO

Every winter, millions of monarch butterflies migrate from the United States and Canada to a forest in central Mexico. Once spring arrives, female butterflies fly north—but make it only part of the way. They live just long enough to lay the eggs of the next generation, which will continue the journey north. By the following winter, many generations will have lived and died. The butterflies that make the trek south are actually the great-grandchildren of the original butterflies!

EXPLORE NOW!

Many migrating birds rely partly on starlight to guide their way. In recent years, bright city lights have blocked out the stars and caused birds to lose their way. Scientists are encouraging you to help measure light pollution by counting the number of stars that are visible over your city or town. The counts are conducted each October and can be reported on the Great Worldwide Star Count website at windows2universe.org/starcount.

MEET AN EXPLORER

WHO: Daniel Streicker

JOB: Infectious disease ecologist

Much of your work involves protecting bats from disease. Why is this important?

Bats are really important to ecosystems. [They] pollinate plants, disperse seeds, and control insect populations. But like us, bats can catch diseases. Sometimes this threatens bats themselves—like a fungus [called] white-nose syndrome, which is causing bat populations in the U.S. to drop to dangerous levels. Other times, the diseases that bats have can make people, pets, or livestock sick. Being able to prevent them from getting sick would really help both bat conservation and human health. If bats aren't sick, they won't infect us.

How do you know if a bat is sick?

It depends. Rabies is a prominent bat virus that causes bats to change their behavior, become less coordinated, and eventually die. But other viruses seem to have fewer symptoms. In that case, we need to take samples from bats and test them in the laboratory.

To take samples, you have to capture a bat. How do you do this?

We catch bats in the field with a variety of nets and traps, which work because bats can't see the very tiny threads or detect them with echolocation. We put these traps in places where bats are likely to be flying, like along rivers, outside bat caves, or near where bats feed.

What might you do to protect bats from getting sick in the first place?

My team is interested in using a gel that contains a vaccine, which will immunize bats when they lick it off to clean themselves. But bats also will groom each other, so if we cover one bat with the gel, it could vaccinate even individuals that we don't catch. [It's] kind of a self-spreading vaccine. This is still just an idea, but we are excited to try it out.

Do you have a favorite bat species?

I think it would have to be the vampire bat. They have such a terrible reputation because they drink blood, but they are so amazingly well adapted to that lifestyle, which lets them do things that no other bat can. For example, they can hop around like frogs and take off from the ground from a standstill. They have chemicals in their saliva to keep blood flowing, razor-sharp triangular teeth to make tiny wounds, and even the ability to recognize

their favorite animal to feed on by recognizing their breathing patterns.

What advice would you give to a kid who is interested in this line of work?

Studying diseases in wildlife is a great career, and with more appreciation for how important the health of wild animals is for the health of humans and our domestic animals, it is a growing field. I think the key to success is to not get too narrow in your interests. Don't just study one thing about one animal. Study lots of different aspects, from animal behavior, to conservation, to microbiology, to medicine, and even to math and statistics. The exciting things happen when you bridge these fields to answer important questions.

Eco-Challenge

EXPLORERS AREN'T JUST RESPONSIBLE FOR STUDYING WILDLIFE. They look for ways to protect animals that are at risk of dying out. Discover the following animals that are in danger of becoming extinct, and learn what's being done to help.

Whooping Crane *Grus americana*

STATUS: Endangered

BACKGROUND: Before the 19th century, there may have been up to 20,000 whooping cranes in North America. But by 1941, only 15 birds remained! Habitat loss and hunting had practically wiped out the entire population.

ACTION: Conservationists worked to preserve the one remaining flock and encourage breeding. Their efforts are paying off slowly. Today, there are more than 214 whooping cranes in the wild.

Blakiston's Fish-Owl *Bubo blakistoni*

STATUS: Endangered

BACKGROUND: Blakiston's fish-owl can be found in the forests of China, Russia, and Japan. The birds spend their time nesting in the hollows of large trees or searching for fish in nearby rivers. Over the years, logging has taken a toll on the owls' habitat. In addition, overfishing has depleted their food supply. Approximately 5,000 Blakiston's fish-owls remain in the wild.

ACTION: Recent conservation efforts—particularly in Japan—have involved building artificial nests for the owls whose habitats have been destroyed.

Blackburn's Sphinx Moth *Manduca blackburni*

STATUS: Endangered

BACKGROUND: Blackburn's sphinx moth can be found only in Hawaii, where it lives in forests that receive less than 50 inches (127 cm) of rainfall annually. Until the mid-1980s, this insect was believed to be extinct. Factors such as forest destruction and introduction of ants and wasps that feed on the insect's eggs were largely to blame.

ACTION: In 1984, a small population of these sphinx moths was discovered on the Hawaiian island of Maui. Scientists are currently studying the moth to find ways to conserve it. And conservationists are planting aiea, a plant on which the insects' larvae have been found.

Yellow-Banded Bumble Bee *Bombus terricola*

STATUS: Vulnerable

BACKGROUND: Until recently, yellow-banded bumble bee populations were found throughout the eastern United States and Canada, and parts of the Midwest. But surveys conducted in 2012 and 2013 showed a severe decline in the number of bees. The culprit might be the Varroa mite—an insect that was accidentally brought to the United States from China more than 20 years ago. Experts say that the mites lay their eggs inside the bodies of developing bees. When the eggs hatch, the newborn mites feed on the bees and eventually kill them.

ACTION: Experts are currently working on ways to get rid of these mites, and to get the government to recognize that this species' population is in decline.

EXPLORE NOW!

You can help protect birds and other winged creatures in many ways. Here are a few:

> Encourage family members to use fertilizers and pesticides that don't contain chemicals that are harmful to birds and other animals.

> Provide a safe haven for bees and other pollinators in the backyard by planting bright-colored flowers to attract them.

> Add a bird feeder to your backyard. Place it away from the bushes, where a hungry predator (like your cat) might pounce on birds. Also, you wouldn't want birds to crash into windows, so make sure the feeders are a safe distance from them. (For instructions on how to make a bird feeder, turn the page.)

Birds in Your Backyard

THERE'S NO BETTER WAY to attract hungry birds than with a bird feeder. All you'll need are some household items and birdseed, which you can buy at a local pet food store.

FEMALE NORTHERN CARDINAL

DID YOU KNOW?

Sunflower seeds attract the widest variety of birds. Common forms include black oil and striped.

BUILD A BIRD FEEDER!

Materials

- A large plastic bottle (rinsed, dried, and label removed)
- Ruler
- Marker
- Utility knife
- Two kitchen spoons
- One small screw eye
- Twine
- Birdseed
- Funnel
- Adult supervision

Steps

1. With a ruler, measure two inches (5 cm) from the bottom of the bottle. Draw an "X" to mark the spot with a marker.

2. Measure four inches (10 cm) above the X. Draw an "O" to mark the spot.

3. Repeat Steps 1 and 2 on the opposite side of the bottle.

4. Have an adult use a utility knife to puncture a hole in each X and O that you drew.

5. Grab a wooden spoon and insert it through the two Xs. An end of the spoon should be sticking out from two sides of the bottle.

6. Grab your remaining wooden spoon and insert it through the two Os. The two spoons will be perches for the visiting birds.

7. Remove the cap from the bottle. Once again, ask an adult to use the utility knife to create a small hole—this time, in the center of the cap.

8. Take a screw eye and twist it into the hole.

9. Place a funnel into the open bottle. Then pour your birdseed inside. There should be some birdseed on the spoons.

10. Twist the cap of the bottle back on. Then take a piece of twine and run it through the screw eye.

11. Hang your bird feeder by tying the twine around a tree branch.

EXPLORE
Distant Worlds

AS YOU READ THIS VERY SENTENCE, astronomers and other space scientists are making plans and building devices to explore distant worlds. Some scientists are actually in space now, conducting experiments aboard the International Space Station (ISS), a research lab that orbits Earth. These experiments, which include growing food and studying the effects of weightlessness on the human body, are intended to prepare astronauts for extended space missions to other planets and beyond. You'll read more about these planned missions on the following pages.

HELP WANTED

If you're interested in a career in space exploration, there are many options to consider. Here are a few:

ASTRONOMER

Responsibilities: Astronomers observe the heavenly bodies, such as planets, stars, and asteroids, through powerful telescopes and satellite images. During these observations, they collect data that include descriptions of planets and measurements of their positions, which they use to develop theories about these bodies and the universe.

Workplace: Universities, government agencies, observatories, museums, and planetariums

What you need: A degree in astronomy, physics, or a relevant field such as engineering

ASTROGEOLOGIST

Responsibilities: Astrogeologists study the terrain and composition of planets, asteroids, moons, and other bodies in space.

Workplace: Governments, scientific research companies, museums, and planetariums

What you need: A degree in geology, astronomy, astrophysics, math, or another similar field

BE A ... SPACE ACE!

Have you ever dreamed of being a space explorer? You don't have to travel millions of miles to explore distant worlds. You can observe planets, stars, and other phenomenon such as meteor showers and comets from your own backyard. Here's how to get started.

Materials

- Telescope (If you don't have one, you can make one. See page 141.)
- Starry night
- Guidebook of the solar system
- Calendar

Steps

1. What can you expect to see in the night sky? That depends partly on where you live. People who live in the Southern Hemisphere often see objects that aren't visible to people who live in the Northern Hemisphere, and vice versa. Another factor is the time of the year. During Earth's yearlong trip around the sun, different stars and other space objects will be visible. For an idea of what you can expect to see, determine your location and the date. Using that information, consult a guidebook of the solar system for a map of the night sky that applies to you.

2. Pick a good time. A full moon is very bright, which can make it hard to see faint objects in the sky. So choose a night when the moon isn't full if you want to observe the stars and planets.

3. Choose your observation site wisely. Wide, open fields or places that don't have tall structures blocking the view are usually best. In cities, the light from buildings can affect your ability to see the stars. If you live in an urban area, go to a park with a large, open field.

4. Keep a log of all the things you observe, and review each time you go stargazing. Over several weeks, this will help you notice objects that you didn't see earlier.

5. Dress appropriately. If you're planning to stargaze for several hours, make sure you wear comfortable clothes. Always bring an adult!

ASTRONAUT

Responsibilities: Astronauts travel to space, where they perform various experiments, release and capture satellites, and build and repair research facilities.

Workplace: Government agencies

What you need: Excellent health, a love of adventure, and an ability to work in tight quarters for long periods of time. Good math and science skills and a degree in astrophysics, physics, astronomy, or other related field are a must.

ROBOTICS ENGINEER

Responsibilities: Robotics engineers design and create robots to perform tasks that humans cannot do. These robots may work alongside astronauts or they may explore places—such as planets—that humans cannot yet visit.

Workplace: Military, scientific and technical services companies

What you need: An interest in how things work, good problem-solving skills, and a degree in electronics engineering or mechanical engineering

Space Exploration

IN 1961, RUSSIAN COSMONAUT YURI GAGARIN became the first person to orbit Earth. Since then, humans have traveled to the moon, built a research facility that orbits the planet, and even sent robots to Mars. But the age of space exploration is still in its early stages. Discover other missions that scientists have planned or that are currently under way.

New Horizons: Pluto and Beyond

BACKGROUND: The Kuiper belt—a disk-shaped region located just past Neptune—is home to many small space objects, including dwarf planets like Pluto.

THE MISSION: In 2006, NASA launched the New Horizons spacecraft to explore the region. The trek took nine years, but it was worth the wait. The craft gathered important data about the composition of Pluto's atmosphere. It also took photos of Pluto and its moons. Some of the photos showed a heart-shaped region of ice on the dwarf planet!

DID YOU KNOW?

Dwarf planets are objects that orbit a star and have enough mass for their gravity to mold them into a rounded shape. But unlike regular planets, they share their orbits around the sun with other objects, such as comets and asteroids.

Solar Orbiter: The Sun

BACKGROUND: Scientists have many unanswered questions about the sun: Why is its outer atmosphere 1.8 million degrees Fahrenheit (1 million degrees C) , while its surface is a much cooler 10,832 degrees Fahrenheit (6,000 degrees Celsius)? What causes solar wind—the stream of electrically charged particles that is ejected from the sun to the far reaches of the solar system?

THE MISSION: To get to the bottom of these mysteries and more, scientists at the European Space Agency and NASA are currently working on Solar Orbiter, a satellite that is expected to launch by 2018.

Hubble: The Solar System and Beyond

BACKGROUND: Earth's atmosphere can make it difficult to get a clear picture of celestial objects from the planet's surface. To solve this problem, NASA launched the Hubble Space Telescope into orbit in 1990.

THE MISSION: This state-of-the art telescope is one of the largest ever built. Since its launch, HST has captured images of nearby galaxies and young stars that will eventually become the center of future solar systems.

Curiosity: The Martian

BACKGROUND: Scientists hope to one day send humans to Mars, but before that can happen, they need to understand the planet's features and history. In 2011, scientists sent a robotic rover—Curiosity—to explore and gather data about Earth's neighbor.

THE MISSION: Although not the first rover to explore Mars, Curiosity has made some impressive finds. The biggest so far has been evidence of an ancient freshwater lake, which suggests that life may have once been possible on Mars.

OSIRIS-REx: Asteroid Hunter

BACKGROUND: At any given time, countless objects are zipping through space. This includes asteroids, meteors, and comets. Occasionally, some of those objects crash into Earth. Most don't cause too much damage, but some can be catastrophic. (One asteroid is believed to have wiped out the dinosaurs!)

THE MISSION: To prevent something like this from happening again, scientists plan to send a satellite called OSIRIS-REx on a mission in 2016. OSIRIS-REx will collect samples from an asteroid named Bennu, which may strike Earth in a hundred years or so. By studying the samples, scientists can determine the asteroid's composition—and come up with ways to deflect or destroy it if it becomes a problem.

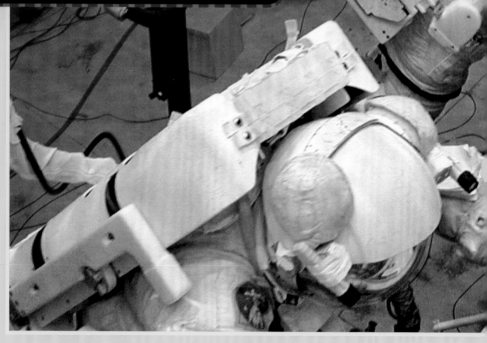

Train Like an Astronaut

BEFORE ASTRONAUTS CAN BLAST OFF INTO SPACE, they go through rigorous training that tests their strength, endurance, and ability to perform various tasks. Do you have what it takes to be an astronaut? Grab a friend and try the following activities to find out.

DID YOU KNOW?

Astronauts who remain in space for long periods of time have to stay in shape. Crew members aboard the International Space Station work out on treadmills and cycling machines—similar to fitness equipment on Earth. But there is one big difference: Astronauts have to be strapped to the machines to keep from floating away!

TOOL CHALLENGE

Astronauts sometimes perform space walks to assemble or repair structures. During these space walks they wear bulky space suits, which can make holding tools a challenge. How do you think you'd measure up? Try this astronaut assembly activity to find out.

Materials

- A small puzzle (no more than 24 pieces)
- A pair of rubber dishwashing gloves
- A partner
- A stopwatch

Steps

1. Dump the puzzle pieces on the floor. Make sure they are out of order.
2. Put on the dishwashing gloves.
3. Have a partner keep time with a stopwatch. When your partner says "Go!" begin assembling the puzzle.
4. When you are finished, have your partner record the time.
5. Switch places with your friend. Have him or her complete the puzzle while you keep time.

AGILITY TEST

Astronauts in space experience a gravity-free environment. This can take a toll on muscle mass and agility. To keep healthy aboard a spacecraft, astronauts must spend time exercising every day.

Materials

- Traffic cones (if you don't have cones, use shoe boxes)
- A stopwatch
- A tape measure
- A partner
- A field

Steps

1. Set up your course. Place your cones in a row. Space the cones five feet (1.5 m) apart.
2. Walk to the front of the row and lie down on your stomach, facing the first cone. Have a partner keep time with a stopwatch. When your friend says "Go!" get up and run in a zigzag pattern, turning at each cone. Try not to knock down any cones. When you get to the end of the row, run back the same way.
3. When you finish, have your friend record the time.
4. Rest for one minute. Then repeat Steps 2 and 3.
5. Rest for one minute. Then repeat Steps 2 and 3 again.
6. Switch places with your friend. Have him or her run the course while you keep time.

ON LOCATION
Welcome to Mars

GOVERNMENT SPACE AGENCIES AND PRIVATE COMPANIES are already planning to send people to Mars in the next 20 years. Although conditions on the planet aren't suitable for humans, scientists are researching ways to make the red planet livable. Check out these pages to learn how.

Gas Factories

Greenhouse gases, like carbon dioxide, are bad news on Earth because they create a blanket around the planet. This blanket traps the sun's rays, causing the planet to heat up. But on Mars, these gases would be welcome. Why? Although daytime temperatures on Mars can be as warm as 70°F (21°C), they can dip as low as minus 195°F (-126°C) in some areas! So, having factories create greenhouse gases on Mars might help warm the planet.

Space Suit

The Martian atmosphere contains less than 0.2 percent oxygen. By contrast, Earth's atmosphere contains 21 percent. So, if humans tried to breathe, they would likely suffocate. Therefore, a space suit equipped with an oxygen tank would be essential. The suit would also protect humans from dangerous radiation and would keep them warm at night.

AN ARTISTIC RENDERING OF WHAT LIFE ON MARS MIGHT LOOK LIKE

	EARTH	MARS
Rotation Period (Day)	24 hours	24.65 hours
Revolution Period (Year)	365 days	687 days
Average Temperature	59°F (15°C)	-81°F (-63°C)
Atmospheric Pressure	1.013 millibars	6 millibars
Average Distance From Sun	93 million miles (150 million km)	142 million miles (229 million km)
Tilt of Axis	23.5°	25°
Gravity	1 g	0.4 g

Greenhouses

Although explorers would feast on prepackaged meals during their trip to Mars, they would need to grow their own food if they planned to stay on Mars long term. To do this, a greenhouse would be built to mimic growing conditions on Earth. Humans would use their own waste to fertilize the crops, while carbon dioxide—a gas that plants need to survive—would be taken from the planet's atmosphere.

Habitat Module

Mars colonists would live in habitat modules they build themselves. Recently, NASA began exploring ways to use 3-D printing to create such housing. This technology uses metals, plastic, and other materials to print three-dimensional objects. Colonists on Mars would likely load their printers with iron from the planet's soil, and use it to print large metal domes, where they would live.

Rovers

In addition to exploring regions that might be unsafe for humans, rovers might be used to tap into water. Scientists recently learned that Martian soil contains about 2 percent water. The rovers could deposit soil samples into a water extractor. The extractor would then heat the soil, causing the water to evaporate or change to a gas. The evaporated water would then condense, or change to liquid drops, which humans could collect.

EXPLORE NOW!

Suppose you are chosen to be one of the first human explorers on Mars. If you were to live on Mars for one year, what would you take with you?

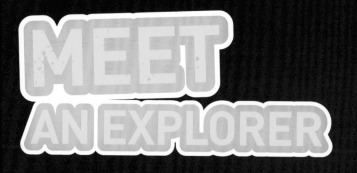

MEET AN EXPLORER

WHO: Kevin Hand
JOB: Astrobiologist

Although many scientists have set their sights on exploring Mars, astrobiologist Kevin Hand is interested in Earth's more distant neighbor: Europa, a moon that orbits Jupiter. According to Hand, Europa might be the only place in the solar system aside from Earth that harbors life.

Why Europa? It has a lot to do with water. "Part of our motivation is that wherever we've found water on Earth, we've generally found life," says Hand. "And so when we think about our approach to searching for life beyond Earth, it comes down to … water." And according to Hand, Europa may have an enormous ocean of water!

Water World

Hand's suspicions stem from images taken by a NASA spacecraft named Galileo. In the early 1990s, Galileo took many pictures of Jupiter and its four largest moons— including Europa. Some of the pictures show detailed views of the moon's surface.

This includes a thick icy shell that scientists believe is up to nine miles (14 km) thick. And beneath that icy shell? "There's likely a global ocean," states Hand. "It's likely 62 miles (100 km) deep."

Mission: Europa

To find out for sure, Hand and his colleagues at NASA's Jet Propulsion Laboratory (JPL) are developing a new spacecraft that will travel to Europa and Jupiter around 2020. The spacecraft will not only take more images of the moon, but it will also analyze the composition of its surface and atmosphere. "And we'll look for signs of life," adds Hand.

So, what type of life does Hand expect to find? He isn't sure, but he's confident that it won't resemble human life. Rather, the life-forms may be microscopic organisms. "Or we may find some Europan fish!" jokes Hand.

"The fundamental questions we're trying to answer are questions humanity has asked ever since we first gazed into the night sky: What is life and could it exist out there beyond Earth?"

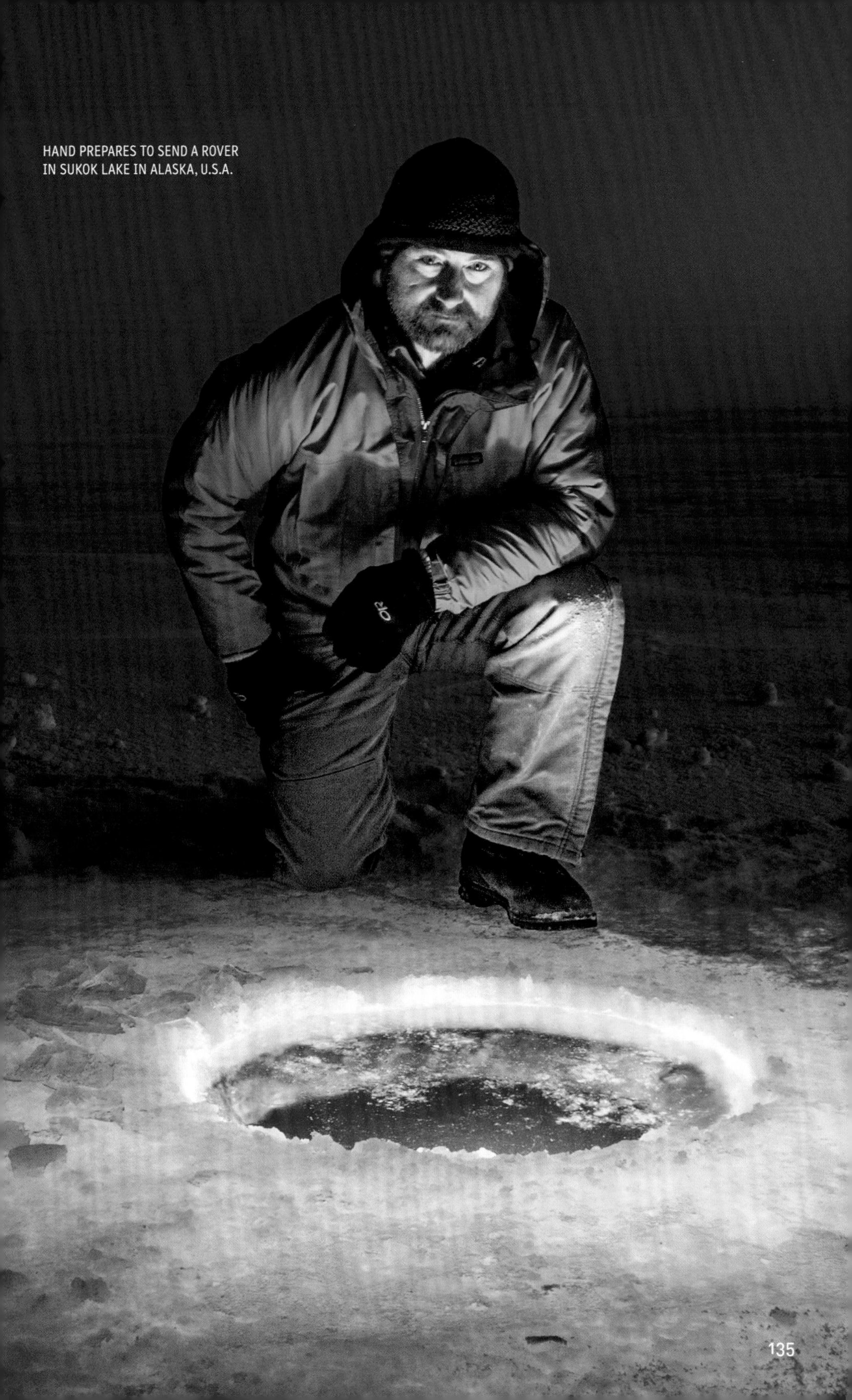

HAND PREPARES TO SEND A ROVER
IN SUKOK LAKE IN ALASKA, U.S.A.

Cosmic Collisions

MANY CELESTIAL OBJECTS IN THE SOLAR SYSTEM—such as the moon and planets—have craters. These are depressions that are often caused by space rocks—such as meteoroids, asteroids, or comets—that have crashed on the celestial object's surface.

DID YOU KNOW?

A crater measuring 5,300 miles (8,530 km) across can be found on Mars. That's almost twice the width of the continental United States! Scientists believe the crater was made when an object larger than Pluto crashed into Mars.

TWO IMPACT CRATERS ON EARTH'S MOON

CREATE CRATERS!

To demonstrate how cosmic collisions work, try the following activity.

Materials

- Newspapers
- Shallow pan
- Yardstick
- Tape
- 6 cups (1.4 kg) salt
- 6 cups (1.4 kg) flour
- Index card
- A large marble
- A small marble
- Ruler

Steps

1. Set the newspapers on the floor in front of a wall. Place the pan against the wall on the newspapers.

2. Place the yardstick upright between the pan and the wall. Tape it to the wall so that it doesn't fall.

3. Fill the pan with flour and salt. Mix the ingredients together. Using an index card, smooth out the top. This represents your planet's surface.

4. Take a large marble. This is your space rock. Hold it two feet (0.6 m) above the surface. Refer to your yardstick for an exact measurement. Then drop it into the pan.

5. Using a ruler, measure the distance across the crater that has formed. Record the measurement.

6. Remove the marble and smooth the top with the index card.

7. Repeat Steps 4 and 5 using the small marble. Record your findings. Which asteroid created a larger crater?

Answer: The larger marble, which represents the larger asteroid, created a larger crater.

EXPLORE
the Sky and You

THROUGHOUT HISTORY PEOPLE HAVE LOOKED TO THE SKY IN WONDER. Many were fascinated by the twinkling of stars. Some wanted to know how birds were able to fly. Others hoped to predict rainfall for their crops.

Although we know the answers to many of these mysteries today, our fascination with the sky is greater than ever. Present-day explorers are constantly looking for faster and more efficient methods of air travel, ways to better predict extreme weather, and more practical uses for technology. You'll discover ways that explorers plan to tackle these issues and more on the pages ahead.

HELP WANTED

The sky's the limit when it comes to careers related to weather and aviation.

AEROSPACE ENGINEER

Responsibilities: Aerospace engineers design, build, and test all types of aircraft and spacecraft, such as airplanes, supersonic jets, missiles, and satellites.

Workplace: Federal governments and companies that develop products for national defense and space

What you need: A love of taking things apart and putting them back together, good problem-solving skills, strong writing abilities, and a degree in engineering

WIND TURBINE TECHNICIAN

Responsibilities: Wind turbine technicians are responsible for maintaining wind turbines—devices that turn wind energy into electricity. They inspect turbines, identify any problems, and make necessary repairs.

Workplace: Utility companies and some organizations that develop commercial and industrial machines

What you need: A degree from a technical school, good problem-solving skills, physical strength, and a love of being outdoors. Because many turbines are at least 260 feet (79 m) high, you cannot be afraid of heights.

BE A ... WEATHER WONDER!

So what does it take to explore the sky? For starters: a little time, patience, and good observation skills. Try your hand at these two simple skygazing weather activities, but always remember: When thunder roars, stay indoors. Thunder means lightning—and lightning is dangerous!

Materials

- Camera
- Sketchbook
- Notebook
- Stopwatch
- Pen or pencil

Steps

1 Keep a cloud journal. Each day, draw a picture or take a photo of the clouds you see. Describe the shape of the clouds and what the weather is like each day. Be as descriptive as possible. Over time, you'll begin to notice connections between the types of clouds present and the weather.

2 If there's a thunderstorm outside, be on alert for lightning. Believe it or not, thunder and lightning occur at the same time. However, light travels faster than sound, so we see the lightning before we hear the thunder. Using this information, you can determine how far away you are from the place lightning struck. Do so by counting the seconds that pass between the time you see a lightning flash and hear thunder. For every 5 seconds, the lightning is a mile (1.6 km) away. So, if you count 15 seconds, the storm is three miles (4.8 km) away.

METEOROLOGIST

Responsibilities: Meteorologists study the atmosphere to make short-term predictions about the weather. They gather and analyze data from satellites, radar, and sensors. Some meteorologists address the public during daily news shows, while others focus on research.

Workplace: Weather and television news stations, federal and local governments, private companies

What you need: A passion for science, good analytical skills, and a degree in meteorology or an atmospheric science

CLIMATOLOGIST

Responsibilities: Climatologists try to predict weather patterns over the course of several months and years. They analyze radar and satellite data, and study conditions in Earth's atmosphere.

Workplace: Federal and state governments, weather stations, agriculture, construction, and insurance companies

What you need: Good computer skills, an ability to analyze data from many sources, and a degree in climatology or an atmospheric science

Seeing Stars

DID YOU KNOW THAT A GREAT DEAL OF HISTORY IS WRITTEN IN THE STARS? Ancient Greeks looked at the sky and saw clusters of stars that resembled heroes and animals from their myths. They named the star clusters, or constellations, after these characters. These constellations are still important today. Astronomers often use them when describing locations of planets and other celestial bodies.

CONSTELLATION ID

So, how well do you know your constellations? Try to identify the following five.

1

The shape of this constellation resembles the horns on this animal's head.

A Greek hero who wields a crossbow is visible in this constellation.

2

3 This constellation looks like a powerful Greek hero who is preparing to strike something with a club.

4 You may have to look hard to see this pattern, but this constellation depicts the body of a winged horse.

5 A large furry mammal can be seen in this constellation.

BONUS: Another famous constellation can be found within the larger constellation. Can you guess what it is?

Answer: 1. Taurus; 2. Orion; 3. Hercules; 4. Pegasus; 5. Ursa Major (the Great Bear); BONUS: the Big Dipper.

LOOK TO THE STARS

Now that you're familiar with these constellations, it's time to go find them in the night sky. You'll need a clear night, an adult, and this homemade telescope to help.

Materials

- Two paper towel tubes
- Scissors
- Masking tape
- Two convex lenses (from an old pair of glasses)

Steps

1. Create the inner tube of the telescope. Have an adult help you use scissors to cut one paper towel tube lengthwise on one side. Curl one side of the cut edge slightly over the other. Then tape the edge down.

2. Insert the inner tube into the other paper towel tube. The inner tube should fit snugly, but still be able to slide in and out of the telescope.

3. Tape one convex lens to the outer end of each tube. Be sure to tape around the edges only.

4. Hold your telescope with the inner tube facing your eye. Point the telescope up at the night sky. (Focus by sliding the inner tube in and out.) Have fun!

Future of Flight

AVIATION HAS COME A LONG WAY since Orville and Wilbur Wright flew the first airplane in Kitty Hawk, North Carolina, U.S.A., in 1903. Engineers are constantly looking for ways to develop new technology and improve existing aircraft. Discover some cutting-edge aircraft and find out what the future of air travel holds.

Drones

BACKGROUND: Drones are aerial vehicles that are remote-controlled by people. This allows the vehicles to fly through areas that are unsafe for human pilots and passengers.

FUTURE: Researchers are developing special drones that can be used for other purposes, such as delivering vaccines and other medicines to remote areas that are too difficult to reach by road.

Aeroscraft ML868

BACKGROUND: In 1852, French engineer Henri Giffard invented the first powered airship, otherwise known as a blimp. Giffard's airship was filled with hydrogen and could travel at six miles an hour (9.7 km/h). Unfortunately, it wasn't very stable and couldn't fly during windy conditions.

FUTURE: Airship design has come a long way since 1852. When the Aeroscraft ML868 is complete, the airship will measure 770 feet (235 m) long. The ship will not only be stable but will also effortlessly carry 250 tons (227 mt) of cargo. The ship will also be able to take off from and land on any surface. It could be used by firefighters in disaster areas or to help transport cargo for the military.

Jet Pack

BACKGROUND: People have been trying to invent practical jet packs for years. However, few devices have ever made it off the ground.

FUTURE: One company in New Zealand is close to making that dream a reality. The Martin Aircraft Company's jet pack relies on two powerful fans powered by a gasoline engine to lift its pilot to an altitude of 3,280 feet (1,000 m). The jet pack may look like a giant toy, but the company hopes emergency first responders will use it to help victims of disasters.

SpaceShipTwo

BACKGROUND: For years, astronauts needed space shuttles to travel to space. To blast into orbit, the shuttle relied on rocket boosters, which carried the orbiter for two minutes before falling off. A single shuttle cost $2 billion to build!

FUTURE: When the new and improved SpaceShipTwo is completed, it will be the first vehicle designed to take tourists to space. With a price tag of $50 million, the spacecraft is cheaper to build than a shuttle. The craft is carried by a jet airplane to the edge of Earth's atmosphere. At 50,000 feet (15,240 m) above Earth's surface, SpaceShipTwo separates from the plane. At that point, the spacecraft pilots fire its engines for 70 seconds and then turn off the ignition to let the craft glide 62 miles (100 km) above the Earth.

EXPLORE NOW!

Suppose you are an aeronautical engineer. What would your craft do? What would it look like? Design your aircraft, drawing on inspiration from the inventions on this page.

The Atmosphere

YOU MAY NOT BE ABLE TO SEE IT, but Earth is surrounded by layers of gases called the atmosphere. Over the years, scientists have discovered important information about each layer. Check out the following diagram to learn about their findings.

Thermosphere

50 TO 400 MILES (80 TO 644 KM) ABOVE EARTH'S SURFACE
The thermosphere is a thin layer, but it absorbs a great deal of radiation from the sun. As a result, temperature here can reach up to 440°F (226°C). The thermosphere is home to nature's most spectacular light shows: the aurora borealis and australis, also known as the northern and southern lights. These lights occur when fast-moving particles called electrons collide with oxygen and nitrogen gas in the atmosphere.

Troposphere

UP TO 5 TO 9 MILES (8 TO 14.5 KM) ABOVE EARTH'S SURFACE
The troposphere is the lowest part of Earth's atmosphere and the layer in which weather occurs. You can also expect to find most airborne birds here, as well as low-flying aircraft, such as helicopters. The temperature of the troposphere is warm near the bottom and cold on top.

Stratosphere

9 TO 31 MILES (14.5 TO 50 KM) ABOVE EARTH'S SURFACE
The stratosphere is home to the ozone layer—a gas that forms a thin, protective layer. The ozone protects Earth from harmful ultraviolet radiation from the sun. Scientists often release weather balloons into this layer to determine wind speed and direction, humidity, air pressure, and temperature.

Exosphere

400 TO 40,000 MILES (644 TO 64,374 KM) ABOVE EARTH'S SURFACE
The exosphere is the uppermost layer of Earth's atmosphere. This layer is extremely thin. Particles floating around in the exosphere drift off into deep space.

Mesosphere

31 TO 50 MILES (50 TO 80 KM) ABOVE EARTH'S SURFACE
Temperatures in the mesosphere dip to a bone-chilling minus 180°F (-117°C). But when space rocks called meteors are zooming toward Earth, they burn up in this layer. Why? When objects are moving through space, they move through a vacuum. But in the mesosphere, the objects encounter gas molecules. As the speeding object rubs against these molecules, it experiences friction and begins to burn as a result. Scientists have insulated spacecraft with special materials such as silica to prevent them from burning up as they enter the atmosphere.

Ionosphere

30 TO 600 MILES (48 TO 965 KM) ABOVE EARTH'S SURFACE
The ionosphere is a layer of ionized gases that overlaps into the mesosphere and thermosphere. Geomagnetic storms that cause changes in this layer can interfere with GPS navigation and high-frequency radio communications.

EXPLORE NOW!

As you approach Earth's surface, the weight of the atmosphere causes air pressure to become greater. You might not be able to feel the pressure, but you can see it in this activity. You'll need to grab a large empty plastic bottle, a balloon, a utility knife, and an adult:

> Ask an adult to use a utility knife to cut a nickel-size hole into the side of the plastic bottle. The hole should be about two inches (5 cm) from the bottom of the bottle.

> Remove the cap from the bottle. Insert the balloon into the top of the bottle. Stretch the mouth of the balloon over the top of the bottle.

> Place your mouth over the mouth of the balloon and blow. Does the balloon inflate?

> Place your mouth over the hole on the side of the bottle. Suck out the air from the bottle. Then watch the balloon blow up! Why is this happening? Air pressure is all around us. When you suck out air from the balloon, air pressure is forced into the mouth of the balloon, causing it to blow up!

145

MEET AN EXPLORER

WHO: Jim Reed

JOB: Extreme weather photographer

Did your experiences as a kid have any influence on your career choice?

When I was around six, I lived in Illinois, U.S.A., with my mother. Illinois had a lot of different weather. We had ice storms, blizzards, tornadoes, and floods. I remember one particular ice storm in 1978 that uprooted some of the trees in our backyard. That left a lasting impression on me.

When did you decide that weather photography would be your specialty?

Years later, I was studying cinema and theater, and making student films. I went on to work in movies and television commercials, and for some reason, these productions always seemed to be disrupted by weather. It felt like someone was trying to tell me that I was focusing on the wrong thing! Eventually I turned my camera up at the sky.

What was your first big experience photographing extreme weather?

I was actually working as a writer for a while. I moved to Wichita, Kansas, to research and write a story about storm chasers. I became so fascinated with it, that instead of just being an interviewer, I started doing it myself.

How do you stay safe?

When I'm out in the field with a crew, I emphasize safety. The first thing is knowledge: understanding what the risk is and minimizing your exposure to that risk. If you're not prepared, it can have disappointing, if not dangerous, consequences. You need to learn and understand the subject. And team up with someone.

Can you share any tips for photographing storms?

If it's raining and you don't hear thunder, I would set up a camera near an open window, a garage, or porch awning. This will help keep the rain off your lens. Then look for something that would help demonstrate the severity of the storm. For example, it could be a person trying to hold an umbrella. It'll help show just how windy or rainy it is. However, if you hear thunder, don't do any of this. Thunder means that lightning is nearby. There's always an element of risk with lightning—even if you're standing behind a window in your house. Even as a professional photographer, I've come close to being hit nearly a few dozen times in my career.

What advice would you give to a kid who wants to become a weather photographer?

Start off by learning about your subject. A lot of National Weather Service offices sponsor spotter talks at the beginning of the storm season. It's a great opportunity to learn more about the weather. Also, take as many pictures as you can—of anything. It helps you become more familiar with your camera, and develop a style.

STORM CHASERS MONITOR A TORNADO IN KANSAS, U.S.A.

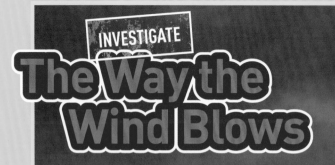

The Way the Wind Blows

METEOROLOGISTS AND OTHER SCIENTISTS monitor the direction of the wind to determine which way a storm is heading. This allows them to warn people who are in the path of the storm.

So, how can you keep track of wind direction? With a wind vane!

LIGHTNING DURING A THUNDERSTORM

MAKE A WIND VANE!

Materials

- Cardboard
- Scissors
- Masking tape
- Empty coffee can (or an empty soup can)
- Unsharpened pencil
- Pen cap that fits loosely over the pencil end
- Sand (or gravel)
- Clay
- Compass
- Marker

Steps

1. Draw the shape of an arrow that measures five inches (12.7 cm) long on the cardboard. Have an adult help you cut out the arrow with scissors.

2. Place the coffee can on the cardboard. Have an adult cut a circle that's a little bigger than the circumference of the can.

3. Use a marker to write the directions north (N), northeast (NE), east (E), southeast (SE), south (S), southwest (SW), west (W), and northwest (NW) on the circle. In the center, poke a hole big enough for the pencil to pass through.

4. With the eraser side first, slide the pencil through the hole. Make a small ball with the clay, stick the eraser into it, and put it in the bottom of the can. Pour some sand (or gravel) into the can to stabilize the pencil.

5. Tape your pen cap to one side of the arrow. Position the arrow on top of the pencil by putting the pen cap on the unsharpened pencil end. The arrow should be level and able to spin freely.

6. Place your weather vane outside on a windy day. Make sure the "N" for "north" is pointing north. If you don't know which direction is north, use a compass. (You can usually find one on a smartphone.)

7. When the wind blows, pay attention to the direction the arrow points, not the direction the wind is blowing. Repeat this over the course of several days.

CAREER QUIZ

IN THIS BOOK, you've read about many different careers in science exploration. But which career is right for you? Take this quiz to find out.

Your ideal vacation is:

a. A wildlife safari in South Africa

b. Space camp in Alabama

c. Snorkeling in the Bahamas

d. Hiking in the Grand Canyon

Aliens have landed on Earth. What's the first thing you would do?

a. Snap a photo to share with the world.

b. Approach the aliens as a spokesperson for all humans.

c. Check out how the spaceship was built.

d. Observe the situation to see how it unfolds.

You're in the mood to watch a classic movie series. What do you choose?

a. Comedy

b. Adventure

c. Science Fiction

d. History

Suppose you're stuck in an elevator. How do you react?

a. Text everyone you know to tell them the news.

b. Awesome! You can't wait to see how the rescue unfolds.

c. Try to figure out what's wrong with the elevator.

d. Freak out. You hate small spaces!

You're most likely to watch a show on:

a. Animal Planet

b. Syfy

c. The Surf Channel

d. The History Channel

What's the most daring water sport you would try?

a. Water-skiing

b. Big-wave surfing

c. Kayaking

d. Chilling out on an inflatable raft

Which superpower would you most like to have?

a. The ability to speak to animals

b. Flight

c. The ability to breathe underwater

d. Time travel

Suppose you work for NASA. The next mission is to Mars. What would your job be?

a. You would report details to the public.

b. You would train the astronauts.

c. You would design the spacecraft.

d. You would be an astronaut.

Which classic science-fair project is a winner in your book?

a. Molding bread

b. Cloud in a jar

c. The floating paper clip

d. The erupting volcano

If you were participating in a group science project, what would you be responsible for?

a. Presenting the project to the class

b. Being the guinea pig in the experiment

c. Designing the experiment

d. Taking notes

ANSWERS:

Purple Questions

Mostly a's: Whether it's animals of the present or dinosaurs from the past, you are wild about wildlife! You'll be most happy working in fields such as zoology, wildlife conservation, biology, or paleontology.

Mostly b's: You've got your head in the clouds (and beyond)—that's for sure. Consider weather-related fields such as meteorology and climatology. Or shoot for the stars with a career in astronomy or astrophysics.

Mostly c's: For you, life is a beach. You'd make a real splash in a water-related field, such as oceanography. If you enjoy searching for old relics, consider maritime archaeology. If aquatic animals are your thing, try marine biology on for size.

Mostly d's: You're most likely to have a blast with the past. If rocks and minerals interest you, you might be happy as a geologist who studies the age of rock formations, an archaeologist who studies ancient relics, or a historian who studies people of the past.

Orange Questions

Mostly a's: For you, communication is key. Nothing makes you happier than keeping everyone in the loop. You can work in any field as a journalist, photographer, or a communications specialist.

Mostly b's: You're a thrill seeker who scoffs at danger. Try exploring caves as a speleologist, volcanoes as a volcanologist, or space as an astronaut.

Mostly c's: You are the gadget geek among your friends. You love having the latest technology and are always trying to figure out how things work. Consider being an engineer in any field or a technician who specializes in submersibles or alternative energy devices.

Mostly d's: Risky scenarios aren't your thing. In fact, you'd probably be the last person on Earth to bungee jump. However, your research and observational skills are unrivaled. Consider a job as a researcher or scientist in a field that involves learning by observing, such as zoology, entomology, or astronomy.

GLOSSARY

acidic Having the properties of an acid, a substance that tastes sour or tends to eat away at other substances

adaptation A change in the body or behavior of a species, often over many generations, making it better able to survive

algae Simple, plantlike organisms that contain a green pigment color, but lack true stems, roots, and leaves

amphibian Cold-blooded animal with a backbone that has moist skin and no scales

aquatic Living all or most of the time in water

artifact Material remains of a culture, such as tools, clothing, or food

asteroid Any of a small number of planetary rocks that are found mainly in the asteroid belt that lies between Mars and Jupiter

atmosphere Layer of gases surrounding a planet or other celestial body

bacteria A single-celled organism

bog A wetland of soft, spongy ground consisting mainly of partially decayed plant matter called peat

breed To reproduce by giving birth to live young or laying eggs

carbon A type of atom that is present in all life

carnivore Organism that eats meat

classify To group organisms based on physical and genetic characteristics

climate Average weather conditions of an area over wan extended period of time

comet A celestial object surrounded by ice and gas that orbits the sun and leaves a trail of debris

crater A bowl-shaped depression, or hollowed-out area, produced by the impact of a meteorite, volcanic activity, or explosion

crust Thick layer of Earth that sits beneath the continents

crustacean Organism that lives mostly in water and has a hard shell and a body divided into segments

crystal A solid with a definite geometric shape, made of atoms arranged in a pattern

current A stream of water moving within another body of water

depression An area that is sunk below or lower than the surrounding areas

desert An area of land that receives less than 10 inches (25 cm) of precipitation a year

dorsal fin Fin on the back of an aquatic animal that helps the animal keep its balance as it moves

drag A force that slows moving objects

ecosystem Community and interactions of living and nonliving things in an area

electron Negatively charged particles

element A substance made from one kind of atom that has its own chemical properties

endangered Relating to an animal or plant that is found in such small numbers that it is at risk of becoming extinct, or no longer existing

evaporate To change from liquid water to water vapor

erosion The gradual wearing away of soil and rock as wind or water break them up and carry them away

extinct No longer existing

fossil The preserved remains or traces of an organism that lived a long time ago

fungus An organism, such as a fruiting body called a mush-room, that produces and releases spores when mature and feeds on organic matter

global warming An increase in Earth's average temperature over time

galaxy Collection of stars, planets, gases, and other celestial bodies bound together by gravity

grassland A large, flat area of land that is covered with grasses and has few trees

gravity Physical force by which objects attract, or pull toward, each other

greenhouse gas A gas in the atmosphere, such as carbon dioxide, water vapor, and ozone, that absorbs the sun's energy reflected by the surface of Earth, warming the atmosphere

groundwater All the water found underneath Earth's surface

habitat A place in nature where an organism lives throughout the year or for shorter periods of time

herbivore Organism that eats mainly plants

hibernate To reduce activity almost to sleeping to conserve food and energy, usually in winter

hydrothermal vent A fissure, or opening, in the seafloor that spews hot fluids and gases

igneous rock Rock formed by the cooling and solidification of hot magma as it moves toward the Earth's surface

invertebrate An organism without a backbone

keratin The bony sheath that makes up some dinosaur horns and the covering of their claws; also makes up your fingernails and toenails

landform A feature on Earth's surface that is part of the terrain

larva An animal in the early stage of development that looks different than how it will look in the adult stage

lift An upward force

magma Hot, molten liquid rock beneath Earth's surface

mammal Warm-blooded animal with hair that gives birth to live offspring and produces milk to feed its young

marine Living in or near the sea

mass Amount of matter in an object

metamorphic rock Rock that has undergone a complete transformation while in its solid form due to intense pressure and heat deep within the Earth

meteor Rocky debris from space that enters Earth's atmosphere

migration Process in which a community of organisms leaves a habitat for part of the year or part of their lives and moves to other habitats that are more hospitable

mineral A substance that occurs in nature and has a certain chemical composition and specific crystal structure

mollusk Animal with a soft body that usually lives inside a hard shell and typically in water

nutrient A substance, such as protein, vitamin, or mineral, needed for good health

observation Something that is learned from watching and measuring

orbit To circle an object

organism An individual living thing, such as a person, plant, or animal

ozone layer A layer in the atmosphere containing the gas ozone, which absorbs most of the sun's ultraviolet radiation

peninsula A piece of land that is almost entirely surrounded by water but is connected to the mainland on one side

plankton Microscopic plant or animal organisms that float in salt water or freshwater

plate Giant, slow-moving rock slabs that make up Earth's crust

pollution Introduction of harmful materials into the environment

population A group of the same kind of organism living in the same environment

predator Animal that hunts other animals for food

pressure Force that is applied to a gas, liquid, or solid

prey Animal that is hunted and eaten by other animals

rain forest A dense forest in which at least 160 inches (406 cm) of rain falls each year

reptile Cold-blooded animal that breathes air, has a backbone, and usually has scales

sediment Small pieces of rock that break off larger rocks that have been weathered and worn away by wind, water, or ice

sedimentary rock Rock formed at the Earth's surface form sediment that has piled up and cemented back together or from the evaporation of water containing sediment

species A group of similar organisms that can reproduce with one another

submersible An underwater vehicle with limited power reserves that must be launched from and recovered by a ship

temperate Characterized by a warm summer and a cool winter; mostly located between the tropics and the polar regions

threatened Likely to be extinct in the near future

trench A long, narrow canyon in the seafloor

tropical Relating to the area on Earth between the Tropic of Cancer and the Tropic of Capricorn, where it is usually warm year-round

tundra A cold, treeless area of the Arctic region with permafrost, a layer of soil that remains frozen through the year

venom Poison fluid made in the bodies of some organisms that is secreted for hunting and protection

vertebrate An organism with a backbone

wetland An area of land that is either covered by water or saturated with water

FIND OUT MORE

LAND

National Wildlife Federation
nwf.org/kids

OLogy from the American Museum of Natural History
amnh.org/explore/ology

Mineralogy4Kids
mineralogy4kids.org

WWF Conservation
wwf.panda.org/about_our_earth/species

National Geographic Visual Encyclopedia of Earth
By Michael Allaby
(National Geographic, 2008)

National Geographic Animal Encyclopedia
By Lucy Spelman
(National Geographic, 2012)

National Geographic Ultimate Explorer Field Guide: Rocks and Minerals
By Nancy Honovich
(National Geographic, 2016)

SEA

NOAA Fun for Kids
oceanservice.noaa.gov/kids

Monterey Bay Aquarium
montereybayaquarium.org/
animals-and-experiences

Ocean Futures Society Kids Cove
oceanfutures.org/learning/kids-cove/
creature-feature

National Geographic Channel's
Titanic: 100 Years
channel.nationalgeographic.com/titanic-100-years

National Geographic Kids Oceans: Dolphins, Sharks, Penguins, and More!
By Johnna Rizzo and Sylvia A. Earle
(National Geographic, 2010)

National Geographic Kids Alien Deep: Revealing the Mysterious Living World at the Bottom of the Ocean
By Bradley Hague
(National Geographic, 2012)

SKY

Smithsonian National Air and Space Museum
airandspace.si.edu/explore-and-learn

Audubon Society: Just for Kids
web4.audubon.org/educate/kids

NASA Kids' Club
http://www.nasa.gov/audience/forkids/
kidsclub/flash/

NASA's Climate Kids
climatekids.nasa.gov/menu/weather-and-climate

National Geographic Kids Welcome to Mars: Making a Home on the Red Planet
By Buzz Aldrin and Marianne Dyson
(National Geographic, 2015)

National Geographic Kids Everything Birds of Prey
By Blake Hoena
(National Geographic, 2015)

INDEX

Illustrations are indicated by **boldface.** If illustrations are included within a page span, the entire span is **boldface.**

INDEX

PHOTO CREDITS

ACKNOWLEDGMENTS & CREDITS

Since 1888, the National Geographic Society has funded more than 12,000 research, exploration, and preservation projects around the world. The Society receives funds from National Geographic Partners LLC, funded in part by your purchase. A portion of the proceeds from this book supports this vital work.

For more information, visit www.natgeo.com/info, call 1-800-647-5463, or write to the following address:

National Geographic Partners
1145 17th Street N.W.
Washington, D.C. 20036-4688 U.S.A.

Visit us online at nationalgeographic.com/books

For librarians and teachers: ngchildrensbooks.org

More for kids from National Geographic:
kids.nationalgeographic.com

For information about special discounts for bulk purchases, please contact National Geographic Books Special Sales: specialsales@natgeo.com

For rights or permissions inquiries, please contact National Geographic Books Subsidiary Rights: bookrights@natgeo.com

Designed by Project Design Company

Art direction by Jim Hiscott, Jr.

Paperback ISBN: 978-1-4263-2709-4
Library Binding ISBN: 978-1-4263-2710-0

Printed in China
16/RRDS/1

The publisher would like to thank Nancy Honovich, author, for bringing exploration to life; Jen Agresta, project manager, for her flawless and always helpful leadership; Paige Towler, project editor, for the project's editorial direction and initial concept; Jim Hiscott, art director, for his unfailing creativity and art direction; Project Design Company, designer, for creating the stunning pages you see before you; Lori Epstein, photo director, for her keen eye and photo direction; Alix Inchausti, production editor, for her efforts to make the book flawless; Michelle Harris, for her skill as fact-checker; Heather McElwain, for her detailed copyedits; and the National Geographic Explorers, whose inspiring discoveries gave this project life.